ESSENTIAL GUIDE
—— to the ——
TABERNACLE

ROSE
PUBLISHING

Published by Rose Publishing
An imprint of Tyndale House Ministries
Carol Stream, Illinois
www.hendricksonrose.com

ISBN 978-1-64938-052-4

Unless otherwise specified, all Scripture was taken from THE HOLY BIBLE: NEW INTERNATIONAL VERSION® NIV®. © 1973, 1978, 1984 by International Bible Society. Used by permission of Zondervan Publishing House. All rights reserved.

Also published as *Rose Guide to the Tabernacle* © 2008 Bristol Works, Inc.

Contributing authors: William Brent Ashby and Benjamín Galán, MTS, ThM

Thanks to Professor Alfred Hoerth, PhD, for his comments and help with this project.

Images provided by Jerry Allison Studios: Illustration of the Tabernacle Courtyard and the Tabernacle Holy Place on pages 44–45, 46, 47, 48, 55, 76–77, 79, 83, 87, 98, 99 and the cover.

Images provided by Stan Stein: Illustration of the Tabernacle and Sinai on pages i, 8–9, 28–29, 99, and the High Priest on pages 94, 101 and the cover.

Some photos used under license from Shutterstock.com.

Printed by RR Donnelley
China
October 2021, First printing

CONTENTS

CONTENTS

THE TABERNACLE

- The Tabernacle was a movable tent that God commanded Moses to build. God gave Moses precise instructions about materials, dimensions, and structure of this tent.

- On the one hand, the Tabernacle was a visible expression of Israel's faith. It represented a fundamental truth and conviction about God: He desires to live among his people.

- On the other hand, the Tabernacle represented God's plan to intervene in human history to fix a broken creation.

- The Tabernacle was a microcosm of God's original intentions for his creation. The Tabernacle encapsulated in miniature the characteristics of God's original design for the world. From the beginning, God showed his desire to dwell with his creation and have a relationship with human beings.

- The Tabernacle is also the answer to the question, "How can a holy God live among corrupted people?" Sin separates us from God, it makes us impure, it corrupts us: "But your iniquities have separated you from your God; your sins have hidden his face from you, so that he will not hear" (Isaiah 59:2). The Tabernacle, the sacred objects and the sacred activities within it help us understand how this holy God has planned to live among us. In addition, it gives insight into what Jesus did for us during his life, his death, and his resurrection.

- Studying the Tabernacle will give us greater appreciation for God's desire to dwell in our midst, help us understand his plan of redemption, and allow us to better understand our calling to be holy.

A panoramic view from the top of Mount Sinai. The rainbow in the background is a reminder of God's presence and faithfulness to his promises.

GOD
WITH US

GOD LIVING WITH HIS PEOPLE

CREATION

In the beginning God created an ordered, harmonious universe. It was a creation where everything had its place and function. It was a beautiful, good, and blessed creation. God also made special creatures: humans. Humans represented God in his creation. In addition, God created humans as relational beings. Humans were meant to relate to God (he walked alongside them), to creation (they were the caretakers of the garden), and to each other (God instituted marriage and family life).

Michelangelo

However, humans rebelled against God. God had created humanity in his image; but being in his image was not enough for them: they wanted to be like God—they wanted to be independent from God, to do with their lives as they pleased. Their rebellion overturned the order of creation. For that reason, God cursed the ground and punished humanity. God expelled humans from the garden. Thus, humanity began a journey away from the presence of God. The order of creation was broken. Relationships were also broken. *Things are not the way they are supposed to be. God no longer strolls alongside us.*

GOD'S SPECIAL PRESENCE

God is present everywhere at all times—omnipresence is the name of this divine attribute. However, the Bible suggests that there are occasions, times and places, when God is especially present. When God's special presence occurs, it can be very good news—in deliverance or blessing; or it can be very bad news—in judgment. This concept is very important for the theme of this book, which highlights many examples of God's special presence.

CAIN AND ABEL

The story of Cain and Abel illustrates well the broken relationships after the Fall: relationships with God, creation, and one another.

Brokenness *with God.* The need for altars and sacrifices to relate to God shows the brokenness in humanity's relationship with him.

Brokenness *with Creation.* "Your brother's blood cries out to me from the ground. Now you are under a curse and driven from the ground" (Genesis 4:10–11).

Brokenness *with each other.* It is the first fratricide, a man killing his brother. Cain was a farmer and Abel was a shepherd. Perhaps to prove his devotion and desire to be in the presence of God, Abel brought God the best of his flock, the first-born. Cain also brought some of his crop to God. God was pleased with Abel's gift and displeased with Cain's.

The sacrifice reveals the heart of the worshiper. Cain's gift was not much of a sacrifice; it did not take an enormous amount of faith and trust to hand over to God some of his fruits and vegetables. Abel trusted God to provide for him. He was demonstrating that by sacrificing a significant portion of his livelihood. He was trusting God instead of that lamb to provide for his daily needs. The gift is not the central issue. It is about how much the gift demonstrates one's reliance upon God and desire to please him. God wants to dwell with people who love and trust him with all of their hearts.

GENESIS 4
"Then the LORD *said to Cain, 'Where is your brother Abel?'"*
(4:9)

NOAH

The story of Noah continues showing the effects of sin in the world. Evil continued to spread, polluting the whole world. That is what God saw in humanity: great evil "and that every inclination of the thoughts of his heart was only evil all the time" (Genesis 6:5). God had created the world as the stage for his relationship with humanity. However, as sin and evil spread, violence grew and the brokenness of relationships grew as well. God's presence this time was for judgment. God's terrible judgment was an act of "un-creation": a flood that destroyed all except Noah and his family. God overturned creation back to a state of chaos and disorder.

GENESIS 9
"... I now establish my covenant with you and with your descendants..." (9:9)

Yet, his grace also came through by granting salvation to Noah's family: "because I have found you righteous in this generation" (Genesis 7:1). At the end of the flood, "God blessed Noah and his sons, saying to them, 'Be fruitful and increase in number and fill the earth'" (Genesis 9:1). These are the same words God said to humans in Genesis 1:22! Noah became like a new Adam. It was a new beginning for humanity.

Edward Hicks

BABEL

In the story of Babel, humans tried to become even more independent from God. They sought to "make a name..." (Genesis 11:4) for themselves by building a tower to the heavens. They were afraid to "be scattered over the face of the whole earth" (Genesis 11:4). However, "the Lord came down to see..." (11:5). God did not need to come down to see. It is an expression related to the special presence of God. In the Bible, when God "comes down" it means he is ready to act in a powerful way, sometimes to bless and other times to judge.

GENESIS 11
"Come, let us build ourselves a city, with a tower that reaches to the heavens, so that we may make a name for ourselves and not be scattered over the face of the whole earth" (11:4)

In judgment, God "scattered humanity over the face of the whole earth" (11:9). He also gave them a name, one they did not expect: Babel, which means "confusion." God had a different plan for humans. Instead of a name, God gave humanity a person: Shem, which in Hebrew means "name." Through Shem's family, Abraham was born (Genesis 11:10–26). Through Abraham, the story of God's people began.

Pieter Bruegel de Oude

ABRAHAM

Genesis 1 began a story of blessing (Genesis 1:22, 28; 2:3). In Genesis 3:17, God cursed the ground. Genesis 12 begins a new history, a history of blessing. God's special presence occurs again with Abraham. God talks to Abraham and promises: "I will make you into a great nation and I will bless you; I will make your name great, and you will be a blessing. I will bless those who bless you, and whoever curses you I will curse; and all peoples on earth will be blessed through you" (Genesis 12:2–3). God relates to Abraham still through sacrifices but two important elements are also present: a covenant and a promise. The covenant is unconditional: God promises to give a land to Abraham's descendants (Genesis 15:18–21).

GENESIS 12–25
"I will make you into a great nation and I will bless you; I will make your name great, and you will be a blessing" (12:2)

The initial promise is to bless Abraham (Genesis 12:2–3). The blessing opposes the curse that resulted from sin.

Isaac Laurent de LaHire

JACOB AT BETHEL

Leopold Willmann

As Jacob headed to Haran to find a wife among his relatives there, he stopped along the way to rest. As he slept, God visited him in a dream. In the dream, God repeated his promise to Abraham to be with Jacob and to make a nation from his descendants. Jacob recognizes that "The Lord is in this place…" (Genesis 28:16). God's presence made the place special. It became a sanctuary because God's presence made the place holy. Years later, God would change Jacob's name to Israel (Genesis 32:28).

JOSEPH

The story of Joseph ends the book of Genesis. It is a story that illustrates the promises God made to Abraham. The story is a roller-coaster of emotions. First, Joseph was Jacob's favorite son. Joseph seemed to have it all. Then he experienced the hatred of his brothers. After throwing Joseph into a pit, his brothers sold him as a slave. Eventually, Joseph ended up in Egypt as a slave (Genesis 37).

GENESIS 28

"How awesome is this place! This is none other than the house of God; this is the gate of heaven" (28:17)

When everything seemed to fall apart, "the Lord was with Joseph…" (Genesis 39:2). Although things did not always go right for Joseph, the Bible repeats that "the Lord was with Joseph" (Genesis 39:2, 39:21, 41:38). God's presence protected Joseph and allowed him to fulfill God's promise to Abraham: Abraham's descendants would be blessed and be a blessing to all the nations (Genesis 12:1–3). Through Joseph's wisdom, all the nations were spared from the terrible famine.

GENESIS 39–50

"You intended to harm me, but God intended it for good to accomplish what is now being done, the saving of many lives" *(50:20)*

When Jacob was on his way to join Joseph in Egypt, God met Jacob once again in a dream. God repeated his promise to Abraham and Jacob himself: "'I am God, the God of your father,' he said. 'Do not be afraid to go down to Egypt, for I will go down to Egypt with you, and I will surely bring you back again'" (Genesis 46:3–4). God's presence is with his people anywhere, at any time, and in any situation!

The Family of Jacob (Israel)

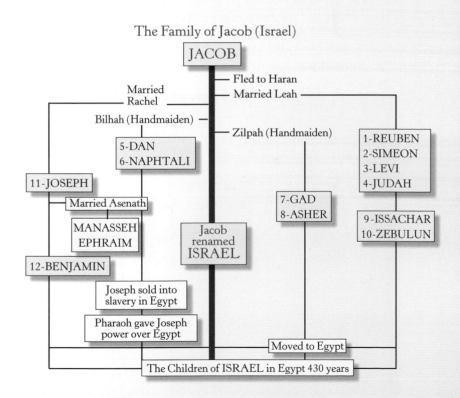

ISRAEL IN EGYPT

MOSES

After Joseph saved Egypt from starvation (Genesis 41), the Israelites lived in Egypt as guests. Eventually, the Egyptians forgot about Joseph and enslaved the Israelites (Exodus 1:6–14). For many years the children of Abraham suffered under Egypt's slavery.

God blessed his people, so they became many. Out of fear from this growth, the Pharaoh issued a decree to kill all Hebrew boys. Within this context, Moses was born to a Hebrew slave family in Egypt. Moses' mother put him in a basket and placed it in the Nile. He was rescued by an Egyptian princess and was raised in the palace.

DEUTERONOMY 34:10–12
Since then, no prophet has risen in Israel like Moses, whom the Lord knew face to face, who did all those miraculous signs and wonders the Lord sent him to do in Egypt— to Pharaoh and to all his officials and to his whole land. For no one has ever shown the mighty power or performed the awesome deeds that Moses did in the sight of all Israel.

Rembrandt

When Moses was 40, he went out to his people. He murdered an Egyptian who was beating a Hebrew slave. Fearing Pharaoh, Moses escaped to Midian, where he was married and became a shepherd.

S. Privezentseva

When Moses was 80, God called to him from a burning bush and commanded him to lead the Israelites out of Egypt. Moses felt inadequate, so God revealed his divine name to Moses and provided him with the ability to perform several miracles to prove his authority.

Moses reluctantly obeyed, and he went to confront the powerful king of Egypt. The Egyptians regarded the Pharaoh as a god, the incarnation of the god Horus. In the eyes of the Egyptians, it was a battle between two gods. The plagues and the Exodus showed that God is the only, sovereign ruler of the universe.

While the plagues demonstrate God's power in judgment, the Passover shows God's mercy and grace. During the last plague, God provided a way for his people to be spared from the killing of the firstborn son. The children of Israel were to sacrifice an animal, which was to take the place of the firstborn from each family.

With a mighty hand, God delivered his people from Egypt. He took them from being slaves to a false god to being servants of the true God of heaven and earth.

The Ten Plagues

The ten plagues were direct attacks against the false gods of Egypt. The following table shows a possible pairing, among many, of plagues and Egyptian gods. However it might have been, it is certain that God was showing that Pharaoh was a false god. Only the LORD is God, and only he is in control of creation, including Egypt.

	The Plagues	God is Supreme
1	Exodus 7:14-25	**Water turning to blood** was a direct attack against the Egyptian god Hapi. The Egyptians relied on Hapi, their god of the Nile, and they probably called on him to provide fresh water. In the end, only God could return the Nile to what it was.
2	Exodus 8:1-15	**Frogs** were important to Egypt as long as they were under control. When God caused frogs to overtake the land, it seemed Heqt, the Egyptian god of the frogs, had lost control of his frogs. Only God could save Egypt from this infestation.
3	Exodus 8:16-19	**Gnats or Lice** swarmed the banks of the Nile. When the gnats/lice became too much to handle, the Egyptians might have called upon Kheper, their insect god, to save them. He could not, so once again, only God could redeem Egypt.
4	Exodus 8:20-32	**Flies** carried diseases. The Egyptians believed that Kheper protected them from these disease-ridden insects. When God caused flies to take over Egypt, the Egyptians probably prayed to Kheper. Only God could end this crisis.

	The Plagues	God is Supreme
5	**Exodus 9:1-7**	Cattle were supposed to be controlled by Apis, the Egyptian bull god. In this plague, all the Egyptian cattle died, but all the Israelite cattle lived. The Egyptians might have prayed to Apis, but he could not save their cattle.
6	**Exodus 9:8-12**	Boils covered the Egyptians, so they probably called on their god of medicine, Imhotep. Once again the boils did not go away, and God proved his power over Imhotep showing all of Egypt that Israel's God is the only true god.
7	**Exodus 9:13-35**	Hail and fire destroyed the Egyptian crops. The Egyptians might have called on Nut, their goddess of the sky, to stop raining destruction on them. Like before, Israel's God, the only true god, could stop this plague.
8	**Exodus 10:1-20**	Locusts infested Egypt and destroyed their crops. The Egyptians probably called on Seth, their god of the crops, to help them. It was becoming clear now that the gods of Egypt were losing to the God of Israel.
9	**Exodus 10:21-29**	Darkness overcame Egypt in this plague. Ra was the chief god of Egypt and was represented by the sun. Ra did nothing to help Egypt because he does not exist. God's triumph over Ra should have humbled Pharaoh, but it didn't.
10	**Exodus 11:1-9**	The firstborn sons were killed in this plague. Pharaoh was considered a god in Egypt, and so was his son. When Pharaoh's firstborn son died, God was proving He is more powerful than Pharaoh. With this, Pharaoh finally relented.

Time Line of the Exodus

c. 1897 BC–1440 BC (or possibly *low date*: c. 1741 BC–1284 BC)

Joseph
c. 1897 BC–1884 BC
(c. 1741 BC–1728 BC)

Joseph is sold into slavery in Egypt by his brothers. He later becomes an official "over all the land of Egypt."

Moses' Birth
c. 1525 BC
(c. 1369 BC)

Moses is born to a Hebrew slave. He is placed in a basket to avoid being killed by Pharaoh. He is rescued by a daughter of Pharaoh and raised as a prince of Egypt.

1850 BC
(1694 BC)

1650 BC
(1494 BC)

Israel in Egypt
c. 1876 BC
(1720 BC)

Jacob, who is also called Israel, moves his entire family to Egypt to be with Joseph. After some time, Israel's descendants (the Israelites) become slaves in Egypt. Their slavery lasts for several centuries.

Some scholars date the Exodus around 1290 BC (low date) and others date it about 156 years earlier 1446 BC (high date).

Key People

Moses

God sent Moses to lead the children of Israel out of Egypt and through the wilderness. Moses was the key figure during the Exodus. He received the Law from God on Mt. Sinai, and is known as the author of the Torah, the first five books of the Old Testament.

Joshua, son of Nun

Joshua was the leader of the military during the Exodus and was one of the two spies to give an encouraging report from Canaan. He led the Israelites into the Promised Land after Moses died. Joshua died and was buried at Timnath Serah in the hill country of Ephraim after conquering the lands of Canaan for Israel.

The Red Sea
c. 1446 BC
(c. 1290 BC)

The people of Israel pass safely through the Red Sea. Pharaoh, the Egyptian army, and 600 chariots are covered by the sea as they pursue the Israelites.

Mt. Sinai
c. 1446 BC–1445 BC
(c. 1290 BC–1289 BC)

After providing food for the Israelites, God gives Moses and the people his law as well as instructions for the Tabernacle on Mt. Sinai. When returning from the top of the mountain, Moses is angered that people are worshiping a golden calf.

1450 BC
(1294 BC)

1440 BC
(1284 BC)

Ten Plagues
c. 1446 BC
(1290 BC)

God sends ten plagues on Egypt leading to Israel's release by Pharaoh and the beginning of the Exodus. The tenth plague is the death of every "firstborn" in Egypt. The Passover feast celebrates Israel's deliverance from death when the angel of the LORD "passes over" their homes because the door posts are covered with the blood of a perfect lamb.

Joseph's Bones
c. 1446 BC
(1290 BC)

Joseph's bones are carried out of Egypt. (An oath had been made to Joseph that when God came to lead Israel to the Promised Land, the Israelites needed to carry Joseph's bones out with them.

Aaron

Aaron was Moses' older brother and spokesperson. Aaron was the first high priest and all high priests after him had to be a descendant of Aaron. Aaron died on Mt. Hor at age 123.

Miriam

Miriam was Moses' older sister. She was the first woman called a prophetess in Scripture. Miriam was an important leader during the Exodus. Like Aaron, she was successful when she supported Moses, but failed when she went against him. She died at Kadesh, just before entering the Promised Land.

Pharaoh

Pharaoh was a king of Egypt and was considered to be a god to the Egyptians. God hardened Pharaoh's heart so he could prove to Pharaoh, Egypt, and the Israelites that he is the only true God.

Old Testament Covenants

The ancient world was very familiar with the concept of royalty. In our day, we have lost sense of what it was like to have a king. We do not fully understand how difficult it was for people to relate to someone so lofty. "Regular" people did not have contact with royalty. A covenant was often the only way to relate to royalty.

There were two main kinds of covenants for that purpose: conditional and unconditional covenants. In conditional covenants, the king claimed complete authority over his subject. In return, the king pledged to offer protection and provision on condition of the subject's loyalty. The subject, on the other hand, pledged loyalty and service to the king, and expected in return the king's protection and favor. Then there is the unconditional covenant. In these, the king pledged a royal favor on behalf of a subject, perhaps to reward a special service to the king. The favor could take different forms; a common form was a royal grant of land.

S. Yates

One of the main metaphors used in the Bible to speak about God is that of the king. God is the Great King, the King of kings. He chose to relate to humans in terms that we could understand. The concept of kingship is an important metaphor to understand our relationship with our Creator.

COVENANT	REFERENCE	TYPE	COMMENTS
Noah	Genesis 9:8–17	Unconditional	God promised not to destroy again his creation: "Never again will all life be cut off by the waters of a flood…" (9:8).
Abraham	Genesis 15:9–21	Unconditional	God promised to give Abraham's descendants the land. The covenant was sealed with an animal sacrifice rite.

COVENANT	REFERENCE	TYPE	COMMENTS
Abraham	Genesis 17	Conditional	God confirmed his covenant with Abraham (17:2) and made a commitment to Abraham ("As for me…" 17:4). He, then, specified Abraham's commitment ("As for you…" 17:9). God reaffirmed his promise of land, and Abraham agreed to keep the sign of the covenant: circumcision.
Sinai	Exodus 19–24	Conditional	God promised to make Israel his people (19:5–6). God also expressed what he expected of Israel: "Now if you obey me fully and keep my covenant…" (19:5).
Phinehas	Numbers 25:10–31	Unconditional	God granted Phinehas, a priest, descendant of Aaron, and his descendants a "covenant of a lasting priesthood…" (25:13).
David	2 Samuel 7:5–16	Unconditional	God promised to preserve David's descendants on the throne of Israel: "The Lord declares to you that the Lord himself will establish a house for you…" (7:11).
New	Jeremiah 31:31–34	Unconditional	God declares that he "will make a new covenant with the house of Israel" (31:31). It establishes a new relationship with his people by writing his law on their hearts.

Mount Sinai

Although the Bible names many places the Israelites passed while in the Sinai Peninsula, we do not know with certainty the location of Mt. Sinai. Based on analysis of the Scriptures, archaeology, and geography, scholars have proposed over a dozen different locations for the mountain. Much hinges on the route the Israelites took from Egypt into the Sinai. The following are some of the most often quoted locations for Mt. Sinai:

- Traditionally the Israelites are thought to have traveled into the southern part of the peninsula, where the following two of the mountains, which have been identified as Mt. Sinai, are found:

  - *Jebel (Mount) Serbal*, where Christians built a monastery in the 4th century, is an early suggestion.

  - *Jebel Musa*, next to Mount Catherine, where Saint Catherine's Monastery was built in the 6th century (see picture at right), has long been the most favored of all candidates.

- Of the northern proposed locations, *Jebel Sin Bisher* in the central west part of the peninsula has drawn some scholarly interest in recent years. Although with very little scholarly interest, *Jebel Helal* has also been proposed as a possible location for Mt. Sinai.

- Also in recent years there has been much publicity surrounding the claim that Mt. Sinai is to be identified with *Jebel el-Lawz* in Saudi Arabia. A team of explorers, who did not have professional archaeological or historical training, claimed this place as the site of Mt. Sinai. However, because of serious problems with the team's use of the Scriptures, various mistakes in their use of archaeological and geographical data and methodology, the scholarly community has raised important objections to the validity of that site.

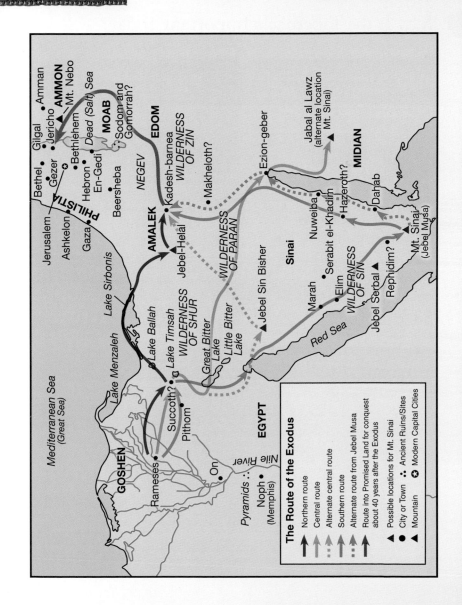

The Route of the Exodus

Why Is the Tabernacle Important Today?

Israelites Communed with God through the Tabernacle	Christians Commune with God through Jesus
1. Bronze altar for sacrifices	Christ's sacrifice
2. Bronze laver for washing	Cleansing through confession
3. Lampstand	Enlightened by the Holy Spirit
4. Table of the bread of the presence	Fed by the living Word
5. Altar of incense	Prayer, communication, intercession
6-7. Through the veil into the Most Holy Place	Entering God's presence boldly through Christ
8. Priest and the garments	Service to God and others

Why is the Tabernacle Important Today?

1. Today, believers are God's dwelling place (1 Corinthians 6:19).

2. God's holy presence is among us (Exodus 40:34–38).

3. As believers, we are part of a priesthood (1 Peter 2:5, 9).

4. The Tabernacle shows a pattern of worship prescribed by God (Hebrews 10:19–25).

THE
TABERNACLE

THE TABERNACLE

THE TABERNACLE CUTAWAY

The Design of the Tabernacle

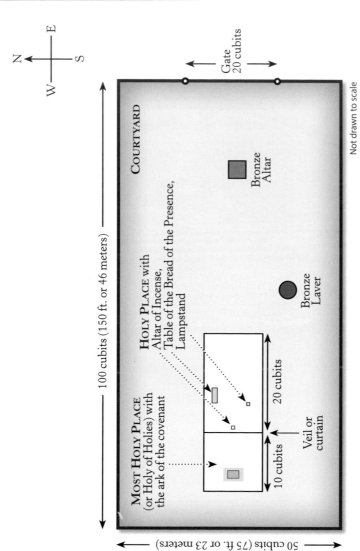

N ← E / S / W

COURTYARD

Gate
20 cubits

100 cubits (150 ft. or 46 meters)

50 cubits (75 ft. or 23 meters)

Not drawn to scale

1 cubit = 1½ feet or 46 centimeters

Bronze Altar

Bronze Laver

MOST HOLY PLACE (or Holy of Holies) with the ark of the covenant

HOLY PLACE with Altar of Incense, Table of the Bread of the Presence, Lampstand

20 cubits

10 cubits

Veil or curtain

THREE PARTS

The Tabernacle had three main sections. Each section contained special, sacred objects. Each section was also the place of different sacred activities.

THE COURTYARD

Sacred objects: The Courtyard is the main access to the Tabernacle. The wide gate is the place where ancient Israelites would bring their sacrifices and offerings. There, the priests would receive and bless people. Within the courtyard, the priests would offer sacrifices at the bronze altar. There was also a bronze laver, in which the priests could cleanse themselves to be ritually clean.

THE HOLY PLACE

The Holy Place housed three important objects for the service of the Tabernacle: The golden lamp, the table of the bread of the presence, and the altar of incense. The priests performed daily tasks inside the Holy Place: they had to keep the lamps burning, offer incense twice a day, and bring fresh bread weekly to the table.

THE MOST HOLY PLACE

The Most Holy Place was a unique place. The ark of the covenant was in this room. God's very presence dwelt in the Most Holy Place. Only the High Priest could enter this room once a year, protected by a cloud of smoke from burnt incense. The most important celebration in the Jewish calendar, the Day of Atonement, had its climax in the Most Holy Place, where the high priest offered the blood of the sacrificed animal to God to atone for the people's sin.

Bible References about the Tabernacle

THE TABERNACLE IN THE WILDERNESS	
Description/Building of:	
Frame	Exodus 26:15–37; 36:20–38
Covering	Exodus 25:5; 26:7–14; 36:14–19
Second Covering	Exodus 25:5; 26:14; 35:7, 23; 36:19; 39:34
Curtains	Exodus 26:1–14, 31–37; 29:9–16; 35:15, 17; 36:8–19, 35, 37
Court	Exodus 27:9–17; 38:9-16, 18; 40:8, 33
Holy Place	Exodus 26:31–37; 40:22–26
Most Holy Place	Exodus 2:3–35; 40:20–21
Tabernacle completed	Exodus 39:32
Dedicated and sanctified	Exodus 40; Numbers 7
Preparation for traveling	Numbers 1:51; 4:5–33; 7:6–9
Names	
Sanctuary	Exodus 25:8
Tent of Meeting	Exodus 27:21
Tent/Tabernacle	Exodus 33:7
Tent of Testimony	Exodus 38:21; Numbers 1:50; 17:7–8
First tent of meeting	Exodus 33:7–11
Pattern revealed by God to Moses	Exodus 25:9; 26:30; 39:32, 42–43
All strangers and unclean are forbidden to enter	Leviticus 15:31; Numbers 1:51; 19:13, 20
Worship and offerings brought to	Leviticus 17:4; Numbers 10:3; 16:19, 42–43; 20:6; 25:6; 31:54; Deuteronomy 12:5–6, 11–14
Trials conducted at	Deuteronomy 17:8–15

THE TABERNACLE IN THE WILDERNESS	
All males to appear before three times a year	Exodus 23:17
Encampment around	Numbers 2
Tabernacle tax	Exodus 30:11–16
Furniture of the Tabernacle and its construction	Exodus 25:10–40; 27:1–8, 19; 37; 38:1–8
THE TABERNACLE IN THE PROMISED LAND	
Names	
Tent/Tabernacle	1 Chronicles 5:5
Tent of Testimony	2 Chronicles 24:6
Temple of the LORD	1 Samuel 3:3
Who shall dwell in God's tent?	Psalm 15
At Gilgal	Joshua 4:18–19
At Shiloh	Joshua 18:1; 19:51; Judges 18:31; 20:18, 26–27; 21:19; 1 Samuel 2:14; 4:2, 4; Jeremiah 7:12, 14
At Nob	1 Samuel 21:1-6
At Gibeon	1 Chronicles 21:29
At Zion	1 Chronicles 15:1; 16:1–2; 2 Chronicles 1:4
Brought to the Temple by Solomon	2 Chronicles 5:5; 1 Kings 8:1, 4–5
TABERNACLE IN THE NEW TESTAMENT	
Tabernacle alluded to (*eskenosen* means dwelt or pitched his tent)	John 1:14
Priestly functions point to Jesus	Hebrews 8:2, 5; 9:1–24

The
Courtyard

ENTERING THE COURTYARD

God revealed to Moses precisely how he should lay out the courtyard. It was 50 cubits by 100 cubits (about 75 feet by 100 feet). The fence was composed of 20 bronze posts on the longer sides. These posts held fine twisted linen 5 cubits (7.5 feet) high by means of silver hooks (Exodus 27:9–11).

ACTIVITIES

Into the Tabernacle Court (Exodus 27:9–19; 40:34–38)
Every Israelite could see the cloud of God's presence over the Tabernacle ("dwelling place"). The curtain at the gate was 7½ feet tall and woven in red, blue, and purple. The courtyard was filled with fire, smoke, bleating animals, bustling workers—and the Tabernacle itself. The Tabernacle was gleaming with gold, silver, and tapestry. Israelites would bring their best animal, perhaps a lamb, as an offering to God.

Sacrifice at the Bronze Altar (Exodus 27:1–8; Lev. 1:1–4)
Once the priest approved the sacrifice, the worshiper would lift it onto the huge 7½ by 7½ foot bronze-covered altar and bind it to the horns on the altar's corners. Solemnly, he laid his hands on the animal's head. The priest caught its blood in a basin below.

The Priest (Exodus 28:1–5, 40; Leviticus 1:5–9; 17:11)
The priest, clad in garments that matched the tapestries, belonged to the line of Aaron, as God ordered. He took the blood and sprinkled some around the altar, then poured the rest below. He cleaned and divided the small animal, then roasted or burned it. As the smoke rose, God accepted the sacrifice. An ordinary Israelite could go no further into the Holy Place.

The Bronze Laver (Exodus 30:17–21; 38:8)
Between the bronze altar and the Tabernacle stood a large, shallow basin of water, gleaming as brightly as a mirror. Priests had to bathe their hands and feet in it before offering sacrifices and before entering the 15-foot-tall Tabernacle and the Holy Place.

The shorter, west side of the fence had 10 bronze posts, as did the eastern side. On the eastern side, the four middle posts held a screen-like gate of special embroidery (Exodus 27:12–19).

Significance	Scripture
• The Tabernacle was God's dwelling place. • The curtains stood for the barrier separating people from a magnificent and holy God. • God could only be approached with repentance and sacrifice.	God with us: Ezekiel 37:26–28; John 1:14; Revelation 21:3 God's majesty: Psalm 29; Psalm 104; Isaiah 66:1 Sin and repentance: Psalm 15:1, 2; Romans 1:18–20; Romans 3:23; Luke 18:9–14
• A proper sacrifice was offering what was valuable and perfect, not unwanted or flawed. • Sin was serious. Only shed blood, which stands for life, could pay for sin. • By laying their hands on it, the Israelites identified with the animal to be sacrificed.	Sin's penalty: Romans 6:23; Hebrews 9:22 Christ died as the sacrifice for sin: Isaiah 53:4–7; John 1:29; Romans 3:22–25; Hebrews 9:13, 14; 1 Peter 1:18, 19; Revelation 5:6–13
• Humans could not approach God on their own but only through his chosen mediator. • The blood paid the penalty for sin. • Heartfelt sacrifice pleased God.	Now Christ is our mediator: 1 Timothy 2:5; Hebrews 12:22–24 Christ's blood paid the penalty: Romans 5:8, 9; Ephesians 1:7; Colossians 1:19–22; 1 Peter 1:1, 2 Loving God is the great commandment: Psalm 51:16, 17; Matthew 22:37–38; Ephesians 5:2
• Washing hands and feet stood for sanctification, or becoming holy and pure. • Serving God requires not just cleansing from sin, but striving for holiness.	Our priestly service: 1 Peter 2:5; Revelation 1:4–6 Holiness: John 13:6–9; James 4:7, 8 Washing through God's Word: John 15:3; John 17:17; Ephesians 5:26

Gates in the Old Testament

In the cultural world of the Old Testament gates—especially city gates—played an important role in the life of the community:

- The city gates were probably the location for a marketplace (2 Kings 7:1).

- The city gate was a place where people settled personal affairs that affected the community. This is reflected, for example, when Abraham wanted to bury Sarah, he attempted to buy a field from Ephron, the Hittite. He appealed to a gathering of Hittites at the gate, "… in the hearing of all the Hittites who had come to the gate of his city" (Genesis 23:10). Also in the story of Ruth and Boaz (Ruth 4:1–2).

- The city gate was also a place where prophets delivered their oracles (2 Kings 22:10; Jeremiah 38:7; Isaiah 29:21; Amos 5:10). Their oracles were public and the city gate was the place for public announcements.

- In addition, the gates were the place where elders and judges would render judgments (Proverbs 31:23; Esther 4:6; 2 Kings 7:3–4). This passage makes this judicial function of the gates very explicit: "his father and mother shall take hold of him and bring him to the elders at the gate of his town…" (Deuteronomy 21:19; 17:5; 22:24; see also Psalm 69:13); the prophet Amos reaffirmed this function: "hate evil and love good, and establish justice in the gate" (Amos 5:15).

Ancient Gates and Gates in the New Testament

When Jesus said, "I am the gate..." (John 10:7, 9), he was referring to the common experience of sheep and shepherds. However, the metaphor that Jesus used is further illuminated when the role of ancient gates is understood.

Jesus provides access to the Father for humanity. He is the bridge that allows humans to reach God. Only through him, humanity is able to find salvation from the penalty of sin, reconciliation with God, purification from a life of sin, and the ability to worship God.

The picture above is an artist's rendition of the Ishtar gate, which was constructed in the sixth century BC by King Nebuchadnezzar II.

The picture shows the gateway that was part of the defensive system of the city of Dan. It dates back to around the time of Abraham. It shows the complex architecture and importance of gates in the ancient world. The gateway is nearly twelve feet high and seventeen feet wide.

THE COURTYARD

Within the courtyard, the first thing encountered was the prominent bronze altar of sacrifice. The fire and smoke of the daily offerings reminded the people that God is a holy God. The altar also demonstrated the necessity of sacrifice and the shedding of blood to enter God's presence. The smells of roasted flesh or grain and the smoke ascending to heaven, along with the very earthy animal smells, marked this area of the courtyard as a place where earth and heaven touched. It was a place where reconciliation began.

The courtyard beyond the altar held the large bronze basin or laver filled with fresh water ("living water" in Hebrew). The basin marked the place of purification for the priests. Purification was a necessary part of the sanctification process—that is, the process of making something or someone holy. It was required for ministry and entrance into the Tabernacle itself. From here the priests could be seen going about their duties of sacrifice and attendance to the daily service in the holy place.

Finally, the Tabernacle itself was situated in the courtyard beyond both the altar and the basin. Only the priests could enter the Tabernacle itself, and then only

the holy place (the outer room of the Tabernacle). The high priest was allowed
to enter the inner room called the Most Holy Place only once a year. The placing
of the Tabernacle in the courtyard illustrated the need for mediation between
God and humanity. Sin has broken humanity's relationship with God. Although
God walked with Adam and Eve in the garden of Eden, after the fall humans
could only relate to God in indirect ways: through sacrifices, priests, and rituals.
Through Christ, our only mediator with the Father, we can relate to God in a
direct, personal way. When Christ comes back, we will be able to relate to God
in an even more direct way, face to face (Revelation 21:3).

THE BRONZE ALTAR

The bronze altar, also known as the altar of burnt offering or the brazen altar, was the large altar that stood in the center court. It was hollow, made of a frame of acacia wood and overlaid bronze. Due to the need for portability, the altar was made with rings and poles that could be inserted through the rings on each corner, allowing it to be carried by the priests. Upon the upper four corners were built projections called horns. The horn is a symbol of power. These horns symbolized God's power over life and death and were points where the blood of the sacrifices was sprinkled. To help keep larger animals from coming off the table, the sacrifices were bound by cords to the points of the altar (Psalm 118: 27-28). No steps were allowed around the device but there was a ledge upon which the priests could stand, if needed.

The dimensions of the altar were 5 cubits square by 3 cubits in height (about 7.5 feet square by 4.5 feet high). It contained a bronze grate midway up the entire assembly. The altar was placed in front of the gate of the Tabernacle so that the altar was the first thing seen upon entering the court.

GOLD, SILVER, AND BRONZE

Where did all these precious metals come from? The amount of gold, silver, and bronze used in the Tabernacle was a considerable fortune. All of these metals came from the Egyptians themselves. God granted Israel to come out of Egypt with a great wealth, not for the people's own enjoyment but for God's own purpose. It was meant to be used for the Tabernacle, for God's own dwelling.

The altar was used for burnt sacrifices, both animal (cattle, sheep, goats, and doves) and meal. Several types of sacrifices were offered:

1. The burnt offering in which the entire animal was consumed by fire;

2. The sin/guilt (trespass) offering, where often a portion of the flesh was reserved for the priests;

3. The peace offering, where the one offering participated in consuming a part of the flesh of the animal;

4. Meal offerings in the form of grain, flour, or loaves, were also offered on the bronze altar. A portion was burned and the rest consumed by the priests. The free will or gift offering was of this type (Leviticus 7:11–18; Numbers 15:1–16), as well as the firstfruits offering (Leviticus 23:4–14).

Only the finest animal—a perfect one—was good enough. God asked them for a perfect, flawless sacrifice because:

- The animal represented an undeserving recipient of a deserved punishment.

- God wanted people to trust in his provision, so he asked that the sacrifice be valuable.

- The perfect animal foreshadowed Jesus, the perfect sacrifice who atones for sin once for all.

A priest receives and blesses the animals the people bring to the gate of the Tabernacle

Utensils

EXODUS 12:35–36
*The Israelites did
as Moses instructed
and asked the
Egyptians for articles
of silver and gold
and for clothing. The
LORD had made the
Egyptians favorably
disposed toward the
people, and they gave
them what they asked
for; so they plundered
the Egyptians.*

The daily worship in the Tabernacle required the participation of many priests. While some received and checked the animals at the gate, others were in charge of the sacrifices and the altar, others cared for the supplies involved in the worship. Priests used many tools to carry on their tasks:

- Shovels to remove the ash from the altar

- Pitchforks to place and move the sacrifices on the altar

- Censers to carry hot coals to the altar of incense inside the Holy Place

- Sprinkling bowls to hold the blood that priests would use for sprinkling on the altar in the courtyard, the incense altar in the Holy Place, or the ark in the Most Holy Place

Sacrifices in the Old Testament

The idea of sacrifice is at the core of the Christian faith. The sacrifice of Jesus Christ is one of the central truths of the gospel. However, this important element of the Christian faith finds its origin and explanation in the sacrificial system of the Old Testament. It is true that Jesus' sacrifice has made obsolete the Old Testament sacrificial system (Hebrews 10:1–18). However, the original readers of the letter to the Hebrews knew and understood the sacrificial system of the Old Testament. From that knowledge, they were able to more fully understand Jesus' work on the cross.

©2003-2008 imageafter

The sacrificial system in the Old Testament is part of the Mosaic Law (in Hebrew, the *Torah*). God *commanded* those sacrifices and rituals. On the one hand, performance and practice of rituals and sacrifices was an act of (1) obedience, (2) trust, and (3) repentance. Obedience occurred by following God's very detailed commands about sacrifices. Trust existed in that God would provide for the animals—animals were expensive, a large portion of people's livelihood. And the sincere expressions of repentance in places like Psalm 51 show the true repentance that often accompanied sacrifices. On the other hand, sacrifices existed because of God's grace. Because of sin, sacrifices were God's merciful provision for Israel so the people could dwell with a holy God.

ATONEMENT

The invention of the English word *atonement* has been attributed to William Tyndale, the English Bible translator in the sixteenth century, to express what Jesus accomplished on the cross: the cancellation of sins and reconciliation of God with humanity. The word has two parts: "at" and "onement." Atonement, then, is God's way to bring reconciliation and restoration to the problem of human sin and its effects.

BLOOD IN THE OLD TESTAMENT

One of the greatest problems for people today with the idea of sacrifice is its inevitable bloodiness. Sacrifice today simply appears primitive and cruel. A brief word about how Old Testament people understood the concept of blood will be helpful for understanding the concept and practice of sacrifice.

The first encounter with blood occurred when Cain struck his brother Abel dead. God voiced the seriousness of Cain's offense: "What have you done? Listen! Your brother's blood cries out to me from the ground" (Genesis 4:10).

In Genesis 9:3–6, God prohibited eating or drinking the blood of animals. The explanation for this prohibition is in Leviticus 17: "For the life of a creature is in the blood, and I have given it to you to make atonement for yourselves on the altar; it is the blood that makes atonement for one's life" (verse 11). The blood of animals had a purpose: atonement.

The question remains: why sacrifice animals? First, remember the Apostle Paul's words regarding sin: "For the wages of sin is death" (Romans 6:23). Second, keep in mind that the regulations for sacrifices occur in the context of the Tabernacle in Leviticus. Animals became substitutes for humans: a life, an innocent life, for another's life, the life of a guilty one. Animal sacrifice, then, was God's gracious provision for humans. The shedding and use of the animal's blood for the purifying or atoning rituals was a reminder for the worshiper that a life had been taken: the cost of sin is high indeed. The sacrifice of an animal allowed the Israelites to dwell alongside God himself as his presence dwelt in the Tabernacle.

Sacrifices in the Tabernacle

SACRIFICE		SIGNIFICANCE
Sin Offering and Guilt Offering (Leviticus 4–6; Numbers 15:1–12) Sin offerings and guilt offerings focused on paying for sin. The sin offerings atoned for sins against God. The guilt offerings addressed sins against others, and included paying damages with interest. Various animals were offered, depending on the person's position and income. Priests and leaders, as examples to others, had to offer larger sacrifices for sin, while the poor offered what they could afford. Blood was sprinkled on the altar, the parts of the animals were burned, often with wine poured on them (drink offering). Other parts were roasted for the priests. Since the priests were full-time Tabernacle workers, sacrificed animals were their main source of food.		**Christ's Offering:** Isaiah 53:10; Matthew 20:28; 2 Corinthians 5:21 **Paying for Damages:** Matthew 5:23, 24; Luke 19:1–10 **Poor:** Luke 2:2–24; 21:1–4 **Leaders as Examples:** 1 Timothy 3:1–7; 5:19, 20 **Providing for Christian Workers:** Philippians 4:18; 1 Corinthians 9:13, 14; 1 Timothy 5:17, 18
Burnt Offering (Leviticus 1) This sacrifice represented complete dedication and surrender to God. The animal, usually an unblemished male, bore the worshiper's sins, and died in his/her place. After the blood was sprinkled on the altar, the animal was completely burned up. None of it was roasted for eating.		**Surrender:** Psalm 51:16, 17; Matthew 26:39; Romans 12:1 **Dedication:** Philippians 2:17; 2 Timothy 4:6–7

SACRIFICE		SIGNIFICANCE
Grain (Meal) Offering (Leviticus 2) This offering was given to God in thankfulness. The people brought fine flour, unleavened cakes, or roasted grain to the priests. The priests burned a symbolic handful at the altar, and could partake of the rest. There was very little ceremony involved.		**Giving:** Matthew 26:6-10; 2 Corinthians 9:7–11 **Praise:** Psalm 100; Hebrews 13:15–16 **Thankfulness:** Psalm 147; Philippians 4:6
Fellowship (Peace) Offering (Leviticus 2; 7:11-21) This offering symbolized fellowship and peace with God through shed blood. After some meat was ceremonially waved and given to the priests, worshipers and their guests could share in the feast as a meal with God.		**God's Peace:** Colossians 1:20; Acts 10:36; Ephesians 2:14. **God's Feast:** Luke 14:15–24; 1 Corinthians 11:17–26; Jude 1:12; Revelation 3:20

Jesus and Sacrifices

- The New Testament reveals that Jesus is the fulfillment of the entire sacrificial system (Hebrews 9:15; 10:12; 14–18). John the Baptist, the gospel writers, Paul, Peter and the writer of Hebrews pointed out the connections between the Mosaic sacrifices and Jesus' sacrificial death.

- John the Baptist was the first to have made the connection at the very beginning of Jesus' public ministry. John recognized that Jesus was the "Lamb of God who takes away the sin of the world" (John 1:29). Thus, he connected Jesus to the sin offering mentioned in Leviticus 4.

- In 2 Corinthians 5:21, Paul's affirmation that Jesus was "made sin" may be an abbreviation for "made a sin offering."

- The evangelists Matthew, Mark and Luke record Jesus himself making the connection between his impending death and the Passover lamb (Matthew 26:26–29; Mark 14:22–24; Luke 22:17).

- Paul is explicit about this in 1 Corinthians 5:7. The Gospel of John linked Jesus' death with the offerings on the Day of Atonement (John 11:49–52). The high priest made offerings for the entire nation before the mercy seat of God. Paul refers to

Lisa Thornberg

these sacrifices on the Day of Atonement in Romans 3:25 when he uses the word *propitiation* or *atonement*. It was the work of Jesus Christ on the cross by which he appeases the wrath of God who would otherwise be offended by our sin and demand that we pay the penalty for it.

- The mystery of Jesus' death on the cross is that this was the voluntary sacrifice of the Son of God.

- Jesus came to earth and lived a sinless life so he would be the perfect sacrifice for the punishment of sin.

- Jesus lived a life of obedience, humility, love, and generosity. During his three-year ministry, Jesus showed God's power over human life and creation itself. –

- He took upon himself the penalty of sin, so that every person can have peace with God.

- On the third day God raised Jesus from the dead, proving that peace and life with God was possible for everyone.

- When people believe and confess that Jesus died for their sins and was raised from the dead, they will find peace and everlasting life with God.

JOHN 3:16
For God so loved the world that he gave his one and only Son, that whoever believes in him shall not perish but have eternal life.

THE BRONZE LAVER

EXODUS 30:17–21; 40:7, 30–32; EPHESIANS 5:26; HEBREWS 10:22

The bronze laver was a large basin of brass, in which Aaron and his sons washed their hands and feet. It was placed between the bronze altar and the Tabernacle tent.

The exact shape and dimensions of the laver are not known. These two pictures show two different artistic renditions of what the bronze laver might have looked liked.

The second object in the courtyard was for the priests only. In fact, the rest of the work was performed by the priests on behalf of the people.

After making the sacrifice, the priest washed himself at the bronze laver. This washing purified the priest and prepared him to enter the Tabernacle. In Exodus 30:20, God says priests had to wash so that they would not die when they entered the Tabernacle.

The bronze laver was made from bronze mirrors donated by the women. The Bible does not describe the laver completely, but perhaps it had a shiny mirrored surface which would help the priest wash thoroughly and to remind him that the LORD sees past the outward appearance, straight into the heart.

Holiness and Purity in the Old Testament

To understand the role of sacrifice and ritual in the Old Testament, the following concepts are helpful.

• *Common*, or ordinary, is the natural state of things in the world. It is the opposite of another important concept:

• *Holy*, or sacred, is a special state. It is powerful and dangerous when treated lightly. When two priests offered unauthorized fire to the LORD in the Tabernacle, they died (Leviticus 10:1–3).

The activity of making a thing or person holy, *sanctification*, occurred by means of a ritual. The act of making or using a holy thing or person for common purposes is the act of *profanation*.

• *Pure*, or clean, is another important concept. There are two kinds of *purity*: ritual purity and moral purity. Most things are ritually pure—except for the naturally impure things (like cadavers) or certain animals (like pigs).

• *Impure*, or polluted, is a powerful and contagious state (Haggai 2:13).

Either contact or an action could contaminate a person or an object and make the person or object ritually impure, unfit. Purification occurred by means of a ritual.

It is within the overlap of "Pure" and "Common" that the divine and human meet. Although God demands holiness from his people (Leviticus 11:44–45, 19:2, 20:7, 26), only he can grant holiness (Leviticus 20:8, 22:9). Yet, the Tabernacle was a testimony that God was willing to meet with people who strived to be pure. Thus, most often he met with common, pure people who brought their sacrifices and worship to the entrance of the Tabernacle.

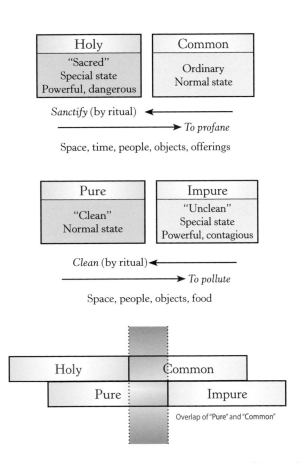

Not every pure thing, or person, is holy. A common person, or thing, can be pure or impure. However, a holy person or thing cannot be holy and impure at the same time. There is a rejection of the impure by the holy. The holy, being powerful, is dangerous for the impure. Thus, the rituals for purification listed in Leviticus were meant as protections not for the holy being, or object (God and the Tabernacle), but for people who were often impure.

Purity, Impurity, and the Tabernacle

The issue of purity was very important for the Israelites. The Tabernacle was at the center of all of Israel's life. God's presence in the midst of the camp determined the life of the people. An important function of the Mosaic Law was to instruct people on how to live in the presence of a holy God. The holy and the impure cannot coexist. Thus, God provided a means to cleanse what had become impure. God chose purification rites and sacrifices to prevent the destruction of the people when they became impure. The following table shows the main causes for ritual and moral impurity and the prescription for achieving purity anew.

Jesus changed this situation. The different purification rites and sacrifices in the Old Testament were anticipations of Christ's ministry. Because of the perfect cleansing in Jesus' blood and his perfect sacrifice on the cross, the purification rites and sacrifices are no longer necessary. For this reason, the causes for ritual impurity listed below no longer apply to Christians.

Ivan Bajic

	Ritual Impurity	**Moral Impurity**
KIND	Unavoidable, since it is part of life. It is not sinful.	Avoidable and directly linked to human sin and disobedience.
CAUSES	1. Entry of foreign entities into the body (Leviticus 11:39–40). 2. Contact with unclean things (Leviticus 11:24–31). 3. Things exiting the body (Leviticus 13:1–46; 15:1–3). 4. Loss of bodily fluids (Leviticus 12:2; 15:16; 15:25).	1. Idolatry (Leviticus 18:21; 19:31). 2. Certain sexual transgressions (Leviticus 18:6–18; 20:11–14).
CONSEQUENCES	Impurity is contagious and inevitable. The Israelites had to be aware of their condition and take the necessary steps to avoid contamination. Impurity excluded people from worshiping at the Tabernacle, or even remaining in the camp.	Moral impurity is not contagious by touch. However, its effects are broad: they contaminate the individual, the land, and the Tabernacle.
DURATION	Temporary and short-term.	Temporary but long-lasting.
UNDOING	Ritual bathing, offering or sacrifice, waiting.	Atonement, punishment, exile, or even death.

TABERNACLE TENT

Just as a fence surrounded the courtyard to protect
those outside of the Tabernacle, a tent protected the
Tabernacle itself. The instructions for making the
tent were very precise in Exodus 26.

Four layers of different
materials covered the tent
from the inside to the outside. The
outermost layer was a badger, porpoise, or sea
cow skin covering. The Hebrew word *tahash* is very
difficult to translate. Most scholars agree that it refers to
the skin of some kind of aquatic animal. As the outer layer, the
leather skin protected the Tabernacle tent from rain or morning dew.

TABERNACLE TENT

Under the outer covering was a covering
of ram skin dyed red.

TABERNACLE TENT

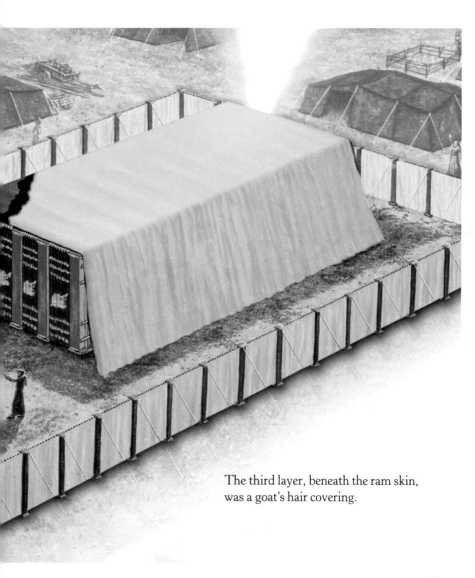

The third layer, beneath the ram skin, was a goat's hair covering.

TABERNACLE TENT

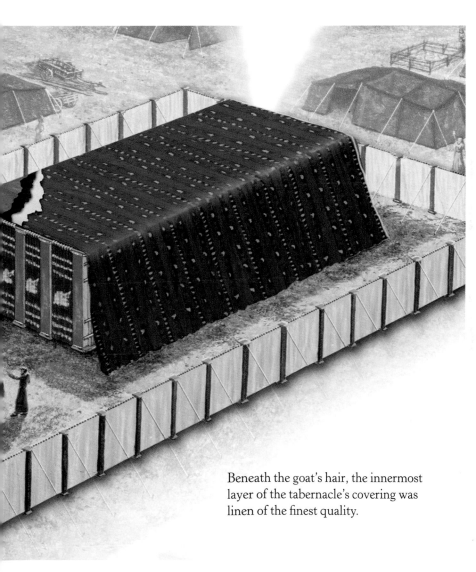

Beneath the goat's hair, the innermost layer of the tabernacle's covering was linen of the finest quality.

TABERNACLE TENT

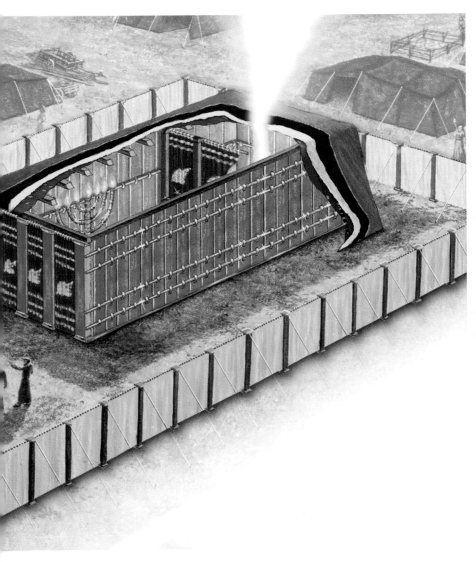

TABERNACLE TENT

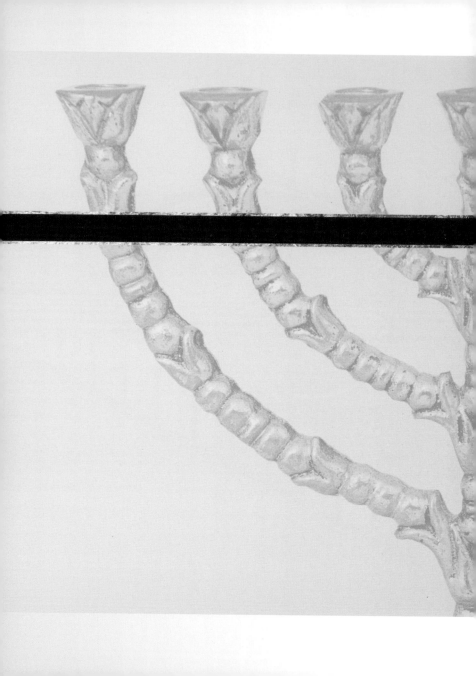

The
Holy Place

The Holy Place

After following the proper cleansing rituals at the laver in the Courtyard, the priest passed through a veil into the Holy Place. This area was holy because of its closeness with the most Holy Place, the place where God's presence resided. It was also holy because God separated this area for special, sacred activities that belonged only to him. These sacred activities used objects that became holy because of their nearness to God's presence. Such holy objects and activities demanded that holy people cared for them. Priests had to cleanse

	TABERNACLE FURNITURE	DESCRIPTION
THE GOLDEN LAMPSTAND	EXODUS 25:31–40; 26:35	The unique lampstand was beaten from a single piece of gold, not pieced together. It was fueled by oil, not wax. It had lamps at the top of each branch, not candles. Its purpose was to provide light in this otherwise dark room. Trimming the lamp wicks to keep them burning brightly was an important job for the priest.
THE ALTAR OF INCENSE	EXODUS 30:1-10	The LORD required that special incense be burned constantly on the altar of incense. It was a special sweet incense, a mixture of spices to be used only for the Tabernacle (see Ex. 30:35–37). No other recipe could be burned on the altar. On the Day of Atonement, the high priest took incense from this altar and brought it into the Most Holy Place.
THE TABLE OF THE BREAD OF THE PRESENCE	EXODUS 25:23–30	On the table of the bread of the presence, Aaron and his sons placed twelve loaves of bread made from fine flour. These twelve loaves represented the twelve tribes of Israel. The table with the loaves was a continual remainder of the everlasting promises, the covenant between God and the children of Israel, and a memorial of God's provision of food. The bread was eaten by Aaron and his sons and was replaced every week.

Tabernacle Symbolism

themselves and offer sacrifices to atone for their own sins so they could perform their duties inside the Holy Place.

The Tabernacle was a place of revelation (Leviticus 1:1). In and through the Tabernacle, God provided guidance for the journey in the wilderness, salvation from the dangers of the journey and sin, and life through provision and his presence. The following table shows some parallelisms between the Tabernacle, Christ's ministry, and the church.

	TABERNACLE	CHRIST	CHURCH
GUIDANCE	God guided the Israelites through the wilderness. By lifting the cloud from the Most Holy Place, God indicated that it was time to move on. When the cloud stopped, the Israelites made their camp.	Christ said, "I am the light of the world" (John 8:12). He is the only way to God. Through his life, death, and resurrection, Christ leads believers to true life.	Jesus said that his followers were to be a light: "You are the light of the world..." (Matthew 5:14). Having the Holy Spirit as our guide, the Church becomes an example of life, a living testimony.
SALVATION	Once a year, the high priest offered an atonement sacrifice, a payment for the sins of the people, and entered the Most Holy Place inside the Tabernacle.	Christ became the only and once for all atonement sacrifice necessary for humanity's sin (Romans 3:25; Hebrews 9:26).	Salvation is through Christ's death on the cross and resurrection. God uses his people to speak about and live the Good News of salvation and repentance.
LIFE	The bread of the presence inside the Holy Place was a reminder of God's covenant with his people and God's provision for his people.	Christ is the bread of life, the life of the world and the source of life (1 John 5:12; John 1:4; 11:25; 14:6; Acts 3:15). By giving his body, Christ gives life to his followers. The bread of communion reminds us of God's provision and promises.	The church is a gathering of people whose lives God has made new through Christ. Christ gives abundant life to his people. The church is Christ's body. When people become part of this body, they find abundant life. The people in the church are the people of the covenant.

THE HOLY PLACE

In this painting, the priests illustrate the three main activities the priests performed in the Holy Place.

1. Care for the lampstand. The priest is filling the lampstand holder cups with high quality olive oil. The lampstand was the primary source of light for the tent.

2. The second priest is pouring incense on the altar of incense. It was a special incense for this special place.

3. The last priest is placing new bread on the table of the bread of the presence. The bread represented the twelve tribes of Israel before the LORD.

THE GOLDEN LAMPSTAND

In the Holy Place, the lampstand provided light for the priests. The lampstand was a solid, one-piece object of gold (Exodus 25:31–40).

God instructed Moses to use one talent (75 pounds) of gold. The gold lampstand was shaped as a central shaft with six branches coming from the sides, three on each side. Each branch held a cup in the shape of an almond flower soon to bloom. Each cup had an oil lamp. It was a piece of art.

Although some translations use the expression *candlestick*, the lampstand did not use wax for fuel. Rather, the lamps used as fuel clear, high-quality olive oil that the Israelites brought as offerings to the Tabernacle (Leviticus 24:2). The priests had to keep the light of the lamps burning continually, probably during both days and nights (Exodus 30:7–8).

EXODUS 30:7–8
Aaron must burn fragrant incense on the altar every morning when he tends the lamps. He must burn incense again when he lights the lamps at twilight so incense will burn regularly before the Lord for the generations to come.

> With the layers of covering on the Tabernacle tent, the lampstand was the only light available inside the Holy Place. Entering the Holy Place must have been an awe-inspiring experience. The light reflecting on the golden objects, shining on the cherubim of the wall coverings and the veil, reflected on the smoke from the altar of incense, must have increased the sense of awe and wonder. The light of the lampstand was a reminder for the priests that God is creator, teacher, guide, and the source of all life.

Although we do not know the exact dimensions of the lampstand, Jewish tradition maintains it was about 5 feet (1.5 meters) high and 3.5 feet (1.05 meters) wide. In addition, the exact shape of the lampstand is not clear. The menorah shape in the picture is only one of different possibilities.

Jesus and Light

By saying "I am the light of the world," Jesus made several claims:

- He is the very presence of God (John 8:58; 1 John 1:1).

- His ministry consisted of guiding people to the Truth (John 8:31–32).

- He brought light and life to those living in darkness and death (John 3:19–21).

In Christ, the full light of God's love and compassion shone forth with power and clarity. Jesus' light reveals our true need for God's forgiveness and shows us the path to God and eternal life. Jesus' light also gives us knowledge of God and his will (2 Corinthians 4:6).

ISAIAH 9:2
The people walking in darkness have seen a great light; on those living in the land of the shadow of death a light has dawned.

JOHN 8:12
I am the light of the world. Whoever follows me will never walk in darkness, but will have the light of life.

REVELATION 21:23
The city does not need the sun nor the moon to shine on it, for the glory of God gives it light, and the Lamb is its lamp.

Hanukkah

ISAIAH 60:19
*The sun will no
more be your light
by day, nor will
the brightness of
the moon shine
on you, for the
Lord will be your
everlasting light,
and your God will
be your glory.*

JOHN 10:22, 23
*Then came
the Feast of
Dedication at
Jerusalem. It was
winter, and Jesus
was in the temple
area walking
in Solomon's
Colonnade.*

The word *hanukkah* means "dedication or consecration."
It refers to the re-dedication of the Temple in Jerusalem.

The events celebrated at *Hanukkah* took place nearly 170
years before Jesus was born. Antiochus "Epiphanes," the
King of Syria, defiled the temple in Jerusalem. He placed
a statue of the Greek god Zeus in the temple and ordered
the Jews to worship it. He also sacrificed a pig inside the
temple—the Old Testament considered pigs unclean
animals (Leviticus 11:7).

This action angered the Jewish people. The priest
Mattathias Maccabee and his sons organized fellow Jews
and fought a series of battles against Antiochus' army. By
a miracle of God the Jews defeated the army of Antiochus
and marched into Jerusalem victorious.

Hanukkah is also known as the Feast of Lights or Feast of
Dedication in the New Testament because of a legendary
miraculous provision of oil for the eternal light in the
Temple. After cleansing the
Temple, the supply of oil to
relight the eternal flame (the
symbol of God's presence)
was only enough for one
day. But God performed a
great miracle, and the flame
burned for the eight days
necessary to purify new oil.

The nine candle
menorah, or candlestick,
called a *hanukkiyah*.

James Steidl

TABLE OF THE BREAD OF PRESENCE

Across from the golden lampstand inside the Holy Place stood the table of the bread of the presence (Exodus 40:22). Priests placed a special bread on the table. God gave specific instructions for the preparation of the bread and the arrangement of the table (Leviticus 24:5–9).

The table of the bread of the presence was another visual reminder of the covenant—the formal agreement that God made with Israel. In the covenant, God promised to be Israel's God and King—in other words, he would protect and provide for Israel; God would fight for Israel and give them a land flowing with milk and honey. Israel, on the other hand, promised to be faithful to God, obedient to his commandments.

Bread and the making of bread are very important metaphors in the Bible. In the cultural world of the Old Testament, people sealed their covenants with a meal (see Genesis 14:18, 18:7, 26:30; Exodus 24:1). The meal formalized the agreement and bound them in a close relationship.

The priests replaced the bread every week during the Sabbath day. God dedicated the bread for the priests, the sons of Aaron. The priests ate this bread. In eating the bread, the priests were representing the twelve tribes of the children of Israel in a covenant meal with God. Such an action was a commemoration of the covenant that God made with the Israelites at Sinai (see Exodus 24:11 for an example of a meal to confirm a covenant).

In addition, the ancient Israelites considered bread as life giving and sustaining. The Old Testament understood that God is the ultimate source of bread and all of life. The

The table was made from acacia wood overlaid with gold. Its dimensions were 3 feet long by 1.5 feet wide by 2.25 feet high (92 cm x 46 cm x 69 cm). The table was fitted with rings in each corner to hold poles for transportation. The poles were also made with acacia wood overlaid with gold. The plates and pitchers that held the bread and drinks were also made of pure gold.

bread of the presence also signified God's covenant provision and presence as Provider for and among the twelve tribes of Israel.

THE DRINK OFFERING
(Exodus 29:40–41; Numbers 28:7–10, 14–15, 24, 31)

On the table in the holy place were the bread of the presence along with plates and pitchers. Priests used the pitchers for the drink offerings, which were poured out on other offerings. In Exodus 29, after Aaron and his sons had been consecrated for serving in the Tabernacle, God instructed them to offer a daily sacrifice along with a drink offering.

Communion

The ultimate fulfillment of all covenant meals is the Last Supper Jesus celebrated with his disciples. The Lord's Supper is a meal that seals God's new covenant with his people (Luke 22:19–20).

The only reference to the new covenant in the Old Testament is in Jeremiah 31:31–34. As God was about to punish Israel for their disloyalty, he also promised to intervene in a new and powerful way. God promised a new covenant—a covenant that contrasted with the covenant at Sinai in at least four things:

Daniele Crespi

1. The LORD will write his law in the minds and hearts of those in the new covenant.
2. The LORD will be their God, and they will be his people.
3. The ones in the new covenant will know the LORD.
4. The LORD will forgive their wickedness.

METAPHOR

A metaphor is a figure of speech in which one thing or person is compared to a specific characteristic of another thing or person using the linking verb "to be."

Metaphors must be carefully interpreted. When Jesus said, "I am the Bread of Life" (John 6:32–35), Jesus is comparing himself with a specific characteristic of bread: it gives and sustains life. Jesus, of course, did not mean that he is exactly like a piece of bread in every sense!

Jesus said that his sacrifice was the fulfillment of the New Covenant. "This is my blood of the covenant, which is poured out for many for the forgiveness of sins" (Matthew 26:28) and "This cup is the new covenant in my blood; do this, whenever you drink it, in remembrance of me" (1 Corinthians 11:25).

Furthermore, Jesus called himself "the bread of life" (John 6:35) because he is the ultimate source of life, both life in general and eternal life.

JEREMIAH 31:31–34
"The time is coming," declares the LORD, "when I will make a new covenant with the house of Israel and with the house of Judah. It will not be like the covenant I made with their forefathers when I took them by the hand to lead them out of Egypt, because they broke my covenant, though I was a husband to them," declares the LORD. "This is the covenant I will make with the house of Israel after that time," declares the LORD. "I will put my law in their minds and write it on their hearts. I will be their God, and they will be my people. No longer will a man teach his neighbor, or a man his brother, saying, 'Know the LORD,' because they will all know me, from the least of them to the greatest," declares the LORD. "For I will forgive their wickedness and will remember their sins no more."

THE ALTAR OF INCENSE

Any priest could offer incense accompanied by some of the grain offering on the altar of incense. It is possible that priests offered incense by itself, although there are no clear indications for this practice (Leviticus 10:1–3; Numbers 16:16–18; Deuteronomy 33:10; 1 Samuel 2:28; Ezekiel 8:10–11).

Priests had to burn incense at the incense altar twice a day—morning and evening—and in connection with two other activities within the Holy Place: the kindling of the golden lamps and the setting of the bread of the presence.

The Day of Atonement was another setting for the use of incense. Once a year, the high priest would offer a special sacrifice and bring a portion of its blood into the most Holy Place. The high priest would also bring incense in a censer from the Holy Place into the most Holy Place.

Made with acacia wood overlaid with gold, the altar of incense— also known as the "gold altar" (Exodus 40:5)— stood in the middle of the western end of the Holy Place. It stood right outside the veil that separated the Holy Place from the Most Holy Place. Its dimensions were 1.5 feet long by 1.5 feet wide by 3 feet high (0.46 m x 46 cm x 92 cm). Although the exact shape is not known, the altar had four horns and rings for the poles.

> The LORD required that special incense be burned constantly on the altar of incense. It was a special sweet incense, a mixture of spices to be used only for the Tabernacle. God specifically required this recipe. None other was to be burned on the altar. The incense was a matter of life and death, as Leviticus 10:1-2 clearly show us, when two of Aaron's sons offered a "strange fire" before the LORD and were struck dead.

EXODUS 30:34–38

Then the Lord said to Moses, "Take fragrant spices—gum resin, onycha and galbanum—and pure frankincense, all in equal amounts, and make a fragrant blend of incense, the work of a perfumer. It is to be salted and pure and sacred. Grind some of it to powder and place it in front of the Testimony in the Tent of Meeting, where I will meet with you. It shall be most holy to you. Do not make any incense with this formula for yourselves; consider it holy to the Lord. Whoever makes any like it to enjoy its fragrance must be cut off from his people."

Jesus, Incense, Prayer, and the Holy Spirit

Incense is important in many religious ceremonies. The ceremonies and rituals that God commanded in the Old Testament are no exception. Like the other sacred objects in the Tabernacle, the Altar of Incense and incense itself had a practical and a symbolic function.

1. The practical function of incense was first to counteract the odors arising from the sacrifices. Sacrifices occurred daily and, on the Day of Atonement, all day long. The smells would have been quite overwhelming, especially for the priests working in the courtyard. In addition, on the Day of Atonement, the incense that the High Priest burned had the function of preventing the death of the priest by covering the Most Holy Place. Thus, the High Priest would not be able to see the glory of God and die (see Leviticus 16:13).

The incense priests used in the altar was pulverized. This picture shows the form of the incense, frankincense, after it was extracted.

2. The symbolic function of the incense is prayer. Like the Tabernacle itself, incense provides a visual reminder of Israel's faith. Just as the smoke of the incense ascends toward God, and the aroma pleases the LORD, so the prayers of God's people ascend to his throne and are pleasing to him (see Psalm 141:2; Revelation 5:8; 8:4).

3. What makes God's people's prayers ascend like fragrant incense? Two important components: The prayer is in Jesus' name, and the intervention of the Holy Spirit. To pray in Jesus' name means to pray in the authority of that name. To pray effectively in Christ's name, we must be "in him"—in union with his life and death.

4. However, the Holy Spirit also plays an important role so our prayers can ascend to God like incense. Jesus promised the gift of the Spirit in the life of his disciples (John 14:16–17) and the Bible tells us that one of the

crucial tasks of the Spirit is to inspire and guide our prayers. When our weaknesses prevent us from relating to God correctly, the Spirit intercedes for us—that is, he pleads our case before God (Romans 8:26–27)—so we can rest assured that the Spirit is praying alongside us, making our prayers what they ought to be. With his help, our prayers can conform to God's will (1 John 5:14).

5. If we understand prayer as communication with God, then we will be able to see it more fully as a dialogue, rather than a monologue on our part. Prayer is a two-way conversation; the other half of our worship before God is God's guidance and clarity of his will to us. Just as we may only reach God in the Spirit through the truth of Christ (John 4:24), so also God's guidance and teaching comes to us only through Christ by means of the Spirit (John 14:26; 15:26; 16:12–14).

Miroslav Tolimir

Intercessors in the Bible

What is an intercessor? In the Bible, an intercessor stood in the gap between God and a people. To intercede is to go between two parties, to plead to one on behalf of the other. In the Old Testament, priests and prophets had this function. They stood in the gap between God and the people. They interceded on behalf of the people. In the New Testament, Jesus is the ultimate and only intercessor that Christians need. He is the Great High Priest.

Why are intercessors necessary? Ezekiel 22:30 says, "I looked for a man among them who would build up the wall and stand before me in the gap on behalf of the land so I would not have to destroy it, but I found none." Intercession was possible because God allowed prophets to know about his plans before they came to be: "Surely the Sovereign LORD does nothing without revealing his plan to his servants the prophets" (Amos 3:7). Intercession is still necessary because of the gap that sin caused between God and humanity. Sin broke humanity's relationship with God, nature, and with each other. Christ is the bridge that joins that gap. Christians can intercede for each other in prayer in the name of Jesus. That is, Jesus is the ultimate intercessor, but through prayer, Christians can also intercede for each other because every Christian is a priest (1 Peter 2:9).

	SCRIPTURE	BACKGROUND	REASON	RESULT
ABRAHAM	Genesis 18:16–33	God had made a covenant with Abraham (Genesis 17). Later, the LORD appeared to Abraham. Three visitors were on their way to Sodom. On their way, the three visitors stopped by Abraham's camp, where they received his hospitality.	The LORD revealed to Abraham that he was about to destroy Sodom and Gomorrah because of their wickedness.	Abraham interceded for the cities and sought God's compassion. God listened to him, though the complete wickedness of the cities moved God to judge them.

	SCRIPTURE	BACKGROUND	REASON	RESULT
MOSES	For Israel: Exodus 32:32; Numbers 14:17; Deut. 9:26. For Miriam: Numbers 12:13.	Moses interceded on behalf of the children of Israel whenever they rebelled against God by complaining, worshiping idols, or opposing Moses and Aaron.	In Exodus 32:32, after Moses' long stay on Mount Sinai, the Israelites lost patience and built an idol—the golden calf. Because of this act of rebellion, God was about to destroy them and told Moses, "Then, I will make you into a great nation" (Exodus 32:10).	Moses interceded with God. Moses appealed to the honor of God's name and to his loyalty to his promises to Abraham, Isaac, and Jacob. As a result, "the LORD relented and did not bring on his people the disaster he had threatened" (Exodus 32:14).
JEREMIAH	Jeremiah 5:1–3; 7:16; 11:14; 14:11.	The people of Israel and its kings became unfaithful and unjust. But they refused to repent and return to the LORD.	The powerful Babylonians were about to destroy Jerusalem and the temple itself. Jeremiah interceded often for the people. However, the people and their rulers remained unrepentant.	Because the people would not repent, God punished them. The Babylonians destroyed the city and the Temple, as well as taking the people into exile. He also promised to restore them in the future.
JESUS	John 17	Although Jesus prayed often for his disciples, the Gospel of John records this long prayer toward the end of his earthly ministry. Now Jesus is the only and ultimate intercessor with the Father on our behalf (Romans 8:34; Hebrews 7:25).	Jesus knew the time for his death, resurrection, and ascension was approaching. The times of sorrow and persecution against the disciples were around the corner. Therefore, Jesus interceded for his disciples and all the ones who would believe by their testimony without the benefit of seeing Jesus.	The coming of the Holy Spirit is a response to this prayer. The Holy Spirit guides believers to all truth, protects us, sanctifies us, and is Jesus' presence within and among us. Christians must intercede for each other in prayer—the Apostle Paul commands it (Ephesians 6:18; 1 Timothy 2:1).

Priests, Levites, and the High Priest

LEVITES	➤ The Levites were one of the twelve tribes of Israel. Levi, the third son of Jacob, was the ancestor of the clan. ➤ This was the tribe of Moses, Aaron and Miriam, which by the time of the Exodus, had grown to a large number. ➤ Because of their zeal to protect the purity and worship of God, the Levites obtained special status as the priestly tribe (Exodus 32:25–29). ➤ There were three families with different responsibilities for the sacred duties. • The family of Gershon was in charge of the Tabernacle, tent curtains and hangings of the court (Numbers 3:25–26). • The family of Kohath was responsible for the furniture of the Tabernacle, including the vessels and the curtains of the inner rooms (Numbers 3:31). • The family of Merari was to oversee the Tabernacle frames, bars, pillars, bases and accessories (verse 36). ➤ God directed the Levites' assistance to the priests at the Tabernacle (Numbers 3:5–10). ➤ In David's time, they helped in the baking of the sacred bread and with the music ministry (1 Chronicles 23:28–29; 15:16).
PRIESTS	➤ The descendants of Levi were the priestly tribe. However, Aaron and his sons were especially separated for the duties of the priesthood. ➤ God's intention was to make the entire nation of Israel a nation of priests to the world (Exodus 19:6). Within that nation, Aaron and his descendants would function as leaders (Exodus 19:22–24; 28:1–29:46). Later, the entire tribe of Levi was dedicated to priestly service (Exodus 32:25–29; Numbers 3:5–10). ➤ The distinction between a regular Levite and one who was of Aaron's line is made clear in Numbers 3:10. • Aaron and his sons were to lead the priesthood and be the ones to approach God. Service in the Tabernacle was an exclusive ministry of Aaron's descendants. • The Levites were responsible to maintain the Tabernacle stocked with animals, grains, wine, wood, and everything necessary for the worship services. They also provided assistance to the priests in the Tabernacle (Numbers 8:18–22; 18:6).

HIGH PRIEST	▶ Only the sons of Aaron could become high priests.
	▶ There was to be one high priest at any given time, but exceptions did occur, such as during the early monarchy when Zadok and Abiathar shared the office (2 Samuel 20:25).
	▶ The office was hereditary and generally fell to the oldest son unless some impediment disqualified him.
	▶ Reasons for disqualification could include moral fault, ritual impurity, or physical deformity (Leviticus 21:10–24).
	▶ Only the high priest could enter the inner sanctuary, the Most Holy Place, to minister before the Mercy Seat on the Day of Atonement once a year.
	▶ The high priest, however, was also in charge of the entire priestly order and involved in superintending the other priests and Levites as well (Numbers 3 and 8:14–22).

THE HIGH PRIEST

WHAT DID A HIGH PRIEST DO?

- God chose the high priest to be the ultimate mediator between God and the Israelites. The high priest needed to be of the priestly tribe of Levi and pure in his lineage as a descendant of Aaron, who was both Moses' brother and the first high priest.

- Being the high priest was not a choice a person could make. It was God who set down the regulations for the office (Hebrews 5:1–5), choosing Aaron and his descendants after him.

- Only the high priest could officiate and conduct certain ceremonies, chiefly the duties assigned for the Day of Atonement. The sacrifices on this day, and most especially the prayers of intercession that took place in the Most Holy Place before the mercy seat, could only be done by the high priest and only on this day in the proper manner.

- The high priest had stricter laws of purity than the people and even regular priests (Leviticus 4:1–12; 21:10–15).

- The high priest, however, was also in charge of the entire priestly order and involved in superintending the other priests and Levites as well (Numbers 3; 8:14–19; 1 Samuel 2:12–36).

Numbers 25 describes how Israel's disobedience resulted in a plague. Phineas, a priest, son of Eleazar, killed the disobedient Israelite. Because of Phineas' faithfulness, God ended the plague. God made a covenant with Phineas. The priestly line would now be through Phineas' descendants (Numbers 25:12).

Zadok, who served under David and became the high priest under Solomon, was a descendant of Phineas (2 Samuel 8:17; 1 Kings 1:8, 45).

GENEALOGY OF THE PRIEST LINE

The high priest, especially, had to be a direct descendant of Aaron. Aaron was Levi's great-grandson. Phineas was Aaron's grandson.

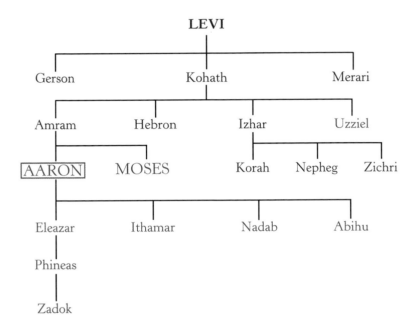

GREAT HIGH PRIEST

When Christ is called our Great High Priest (Hebrews 4:14) it is because he and he alone was chosen by God to make the perfect sacrifice and intercession for us before God's merciful throne—and not before an earthly throne, but before the very throne of God's presence!

Jesus and the High Priest

Jesus Christ is the ultimate go-between (intermediary). He is the connection to God's loving forgiveness and there is none other who can make this connection for us (Hebrew 9:15; 10:11–12). The symbolism of the high priest in the Old

THE HIGH PRIEST ON THE DAY OF ATONEMENT	
The high priest took a young bull and a ram to the altar to offer for himself and two goats for the nation.	
The high priest washed himself in the living (running) water of the bronze laver before putting on his holy garments and offering the sacrifices needed to enter the most Holy Place.	
Entering the Holy Place first, the high priest passed by the table of the bread of presence on one side…	
… and the golden lampstand on the other side.	
Approaching the altar of incense in front of the veil, the high priest took coals and incense and burned them in the Most Holy Place before God in prayer.	
Upon the mercy seat, the high priest sprinkled the blood of the bull and the blood of one of the goats.	
The high priest then sprinkled blood in the Holy Place and upon its furniture.	
The high priest then sprinkled the bronze altar with blood.	

Testament and his symbolic actions illuminate the life and ministry of Christ. Those actions help us to understand better the Gospel of John's presentation of Christ and his ministry.

OLD TESTAMENT	JESUS, OUR GREAT HIGH PRIEST AND SACRIFICE	JOHN'S WRITINGS
Leviticus 16:2–5	Jesus is the Lamb of God and perfect sacrifice.	John 1:29, 36
Exodus 40:30–32; Leviticus 16:4–11	Jesus gives the pure and sanctifying Living Water that cleanses us.	John 4:10–15
Exodus 25:23–30; Leviticus 24:5–9	Jesus is our life-sustaining Bread of Heaven and covenant meal.	John 6:35, 48–51
Exodus 25:31–40; Numbers 8:1–4	Jesus is the Light of the World. He lights our path in the darkness.	John 8:12; 9:5
Lev. 16:12, 13	Jesus, our Great High Priest, has prayed for us before God the Father.	John 17:1–26
Lev. 16:14–16	Jesus is our atonement (Romans 3:25). He offered his own blood on our behalf.	John 20:11–12; 1 John 2:2
Lev. 16:16–17	Jesus ministers in the Holy Place on our behalf.	Rev. 1:12–20
Lev. 16:18–19	The heavenly altar declares God's ways true and just.	Rev. 16:7

Functions of the Priests

A priest is an intermediary—someone who works as a go-between or mediator between two parties. The English language has different words that express this concept: intercessor, arbiter, and advocate. As intercessor, the priest's role had two parts to it. First, priests represented the people to God. Second, they represented God to the people.

1. *The priests represented the people to God* by the many and varied sacrifices required in the covenant God made with Israel at Mt. Sinai.

- Five types of sacrifices are specified in the Bible:

    1. The burnt offering
    2. The sin offering
    3. The guilt offering
    4. The peace offering
    5. The gift/grain offering

- Priests were involved in all of these sacrifices to a greater or lesser degree depending on the regulations.

- Whereas before the covenant, kings and even family heads acted in the role of priests (see, Genesis 8:20; 14:18) the establishment of the Levitical priesthood centralized the role in this tribe and at the Tabernacle/Temple. This also applied to the festival sacrifices such as those at the Passover. Before the priesthood, the household heads sacrificed the lamb (Exodus 12:1–11). Afterward, priests were in charge of sacrifices in the Tabernacle and the Temple (Numbers 16:5–6).

- The clearest example of the priest functioning as representative for the people is that of the high priest on the Day of Atonement (Leviticus 16). On this special day the high priest represented himself, the priesthood of the Levites, and the entire nation.

2. *The priest represented God to the people.* The priesthood functioned as the voice of God—in both teaching and prophetic roles.

- Deuteronomy 33:10 states that the tribe of Levi was to act in a teaching role to the rest of Israel. God placed the instructions, commands, and wisdom of the law in the hands of the priests. Priests taught and guided the leaders and the people about the covenant.

- The prophetic function centered on the use of the Urim and Thummim (Deuteronomy 33:8). What these prophetic devices were is not known, except that they were kept in the pocket of the high priest, who used them to determine God's will in specific cases (Exodus 28:30; Numbers 27:21–23; 1 Samuel 23:1–6). One of the reasons the Levites were scattered among the tribes and received no allotment in the Promised Land was so that they would interact more easily with all the people of Israel in their teaching capacity.

- Finally, the priests blessed the people on behalf of God (see Leviticus 9:22 and Numbers 6:22–27).

3. *The priests also guarded God's sanctuary and guarded the people from the sanctuary.* Holiness can be a dangerous thing for impure people who treat it lightly, as the stories of Nadab and Abihu (Leviticus 10) and Uzzah (2 Samuel 6:6–7) show. The arrangement of the camp makes this protection

clear. The Levites encamped around the Tabernacle, which was in the middle of the camp (Numbers 2:17). They functioned like a fence that protected the Tabernacle from any possible uncleanness from the people. The Levite camp also protected the people who might have become unclean. For such people, the holiness of the Tabernacle was dangerous.

The Garments of the High Priest

Garments of the high priest

- White linen coat or tunic (woven, one piece, close fitting)
- Dark blue woven robe
  - » Reached to knees, hole in it for head, sleeveless
  - » Blue, purple, scarlet pomegranates upon hem; bells of gold between each pomegranate
- *Ephod* of gold, blue, purple, and scarlet entwined in linen
  - » Apron-like, bound at waist by girdle
  - » Shoulder piece coupled together by 2 edges
- Onyx stone enclosed in pouches of gold with names of the 12 tribes engraved on them (6 on each). One on each shoulder of the *ephod*
- Girdle of the *ephod*
  - » Bound around waist, made of same material as *ephod*
  - » Three fingers broad and perhaps reaching almost to floor
- Breastplate of gold, blue, purple, scarlet and fine twined linen doubled, 4-square (around 8-10")
  - » Contained 4 rows of 3 stones (jewels)
  - » Each jewel contained the name of one of the 12 tribes
  - » Set in gold
  - » Two rings of gold were in top ends of the breastplate; 2 chains fastened to these rings, extended up to where they fastened at the shoulder pieces
  - » Two rings of gold were at bottom ends; two rings in the *ephod* above the girdle at the waist laced together with blue lacing; the breastplate contained the Urim and Thummin

Regular Priest's Garments

- White woven coat, one piece, close fitting

- Girdle of fine twined linen with blue, purple, scarlet needlework

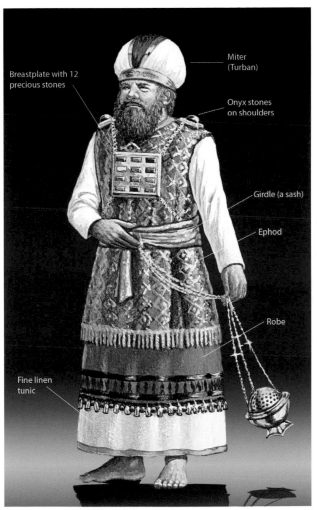

Miter
(Turban)

Breastplate with 12
precious stones

Onyx stones
on shoulders

Girdle (a sash)

Ephod

Robe

Fine linen
tunic

EXODUS 28:2
*Make sacred
garments for your
brother Aaron, to
give him dignity
and honor.*

Miter, Ephod, and Breastplate

THE MITER
The high priest wore a crown of gold, known as a *miter*, which means *wrap* or *roll around*. Sometimes called the "turban," the miter was inscribed with, "Holy to the LORD." The Bible describes two purposes: "It will be on Aaron's forehead, and he will bear the guilt involved in the sacred gifts the Israelites consecrate, whatever their gifts may be. It will be on Aaron's head continually so that they will be acceptable to the LORD" (Exodus 28:38).

קֹדֶשׁ לַיהוה

Holy to the Lord

On the right shoulder

Reuben
Simeon
Levi
Judah
Dan
Naphtali

On the left shoulder

Gad
Asher
Issachar
Zebulun
Joseph
Benjamin

The shoulder stones were chiseled in onyx.

THE EPHOD
It appears to have been a sleeveless vestment. It included two onyx stones, one on each shoulder, inscribed with the names of the twelves sons of Jacob. They were arranged "in the order of their birth..." (Exodus 28:10).

THE BREASTPLATE

Made of gold, it had twelve inlaid stones in four rows. The stones also had names inscribed. However, unlike the names on the onyx stones that were organized by order of birth, the names on the stones were those of the tribes of the children of Israel. They followed the right-to-left order in Hebrew fashion. They were organized following the order of the camp itself. The tribes of Levi and Joseph were not present. Rather, the Levites surrounded the Tabernacle and carried it when they were travelling. Instead of Joseph, his sons, Mannasseh and Ephraim, were listed. The precise names of the precious stones is uncertain, though many translators choose these names.

Zebulun Beryl	Issachar Topaz	Judah Ruby
Gad Diamond	Simeon Sapphire	Reuben Emerald
Benjamin Amethyst	Manasseh Agate	Ephraim Jacinth
Naphtali Jasper	Asher Onyx	Dan Beryl

The names on the breastplate were chiseled on different precious stones.

Most Holy Place

THE VEIL

FUNCTION OF THE VEIL

When Adam and Eve rebelled against God in the Garden of Eden, God expelled them from the garden and placed cherubim to guard the entrance. God's presence was in the garden. Because of sin, humans had become contaminated, impure. The cherubim guarded God's holiness and the tree of life. Humans no longer had access to the garden.

The Tabernacle tent had two rooms: the larger, the Holy Place, was the place of worship, guidance, and covenant. The smaller room was the Most Holy Place—also known as the Holy of Holies. It was in this room that God's presence dwelt.

A veil divided the two rooms. Although priests ministered daily in the Holy Place, only the high priest could enter the Most Holy Place once a year on the Day of Atonement.

The veil was a large curtain made of the finest twisted linen in costly blue, scarlet and purple dye. It was skillfully crafted with representations of cherubim upon it. The veil hung on four pillars of acacia wood by means of hooks (Exodus 26:31–35). Bezaleel and Aholiab were the original inspired artists who headed up the project. Josephus, the Jewish historian, says that the veil was embroidered with

The tall, heavy veil in the Temple was torn from top to bottom at the moment of Jesus' death (Matthew 27:50–51). The veil was thick and the New Testament makes it clear that it tore by itself.

The torn veil symbolizes the free access believers now have through Christ to the presence of God (Hebrews 6:19–20; 10:19–20).

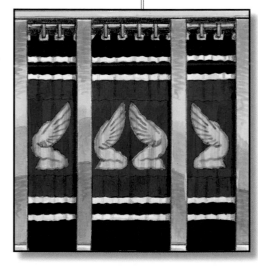

all manner of flowers. Animal forms were prohibited, however (*Antiquities of the Jews* 3:6:4). Some Jewish traditions affirm that the veil of the Temple was as thick as a man's hand. However, no contemporary writer describes the thickness of the veil.

God's special presence was no longer in the garden— rather, it was in the Tabernacle itself! The Most Holy Place, then, represented a memory of what humans lost because of sin, and a hope for what humans could expect with God's plan: living in the presence of God as the Creator intended from the beginning.

CHERUBIM

Cherubim are angelic beings who do God's bidding. They are protectors of God's majesty: they protected the Garden of Eden (Genesis 3:24), they flank or support God's throne (Psalm 80:1; 99:1; Isaiah 37:16; Ezekiel 1:4–28; 10:1–22). They were present in the Tabernacle and the Temple. In the Tabernacle, the Israelites wove cherubim into the curtains covering the inner walls of the Tabernacle tent, as well as in the veil that separated the Holy Place from the Most Holy Place. In addition, God ordered two cherubim to be placed on the "mercy seat," which covered the ark of the covenant. The cherubim appear again in Revelation 4:6–9, where they surround God's throne protecting his majesty.

JESUS AND THE VEIL

	VEIL AS OBSTACLE	VEIL AS MYSTERY
LITERAL	The veil separated the Holy Place and the Most Holy Place.	The veil covered the ark of the covenant, where God's presence dwelt.
SYMBOL	A reminder of humanity's separation from God	The veil reminded Israel that the presence of God is not available for humanity without payment for human sin.
RAISED QUESTION	How do sinful humans relate to a holy God?	How can a holy and just God also be merciful and forgiving?
SOLUTION	God chose the priests as intermediaries between God and the people. Through the priests' prayers, sacrifices, and other rituals, the people could approach and live with a holy God.	God provided a means to seek forgiveness: sacrifice. The sacrificed animal would stand in place of the guilty person, and the result would appease God's justice.

The Apostle Paul called this appeasement of God's anger *atonement*, which he uses to describe what Jesus' death on the cross accomplished (Romans 3:25; 1 John 2:2). Because Jesus completely satisfied the demands of justice, there is now no impediment, no obstacle between God and humanity. Matthew 27:51 says that at the moment of Jesus' death the veil was torn in two. The way to God is again open. Humanity, once again, can dwell in the presence of the Creator.

The apostle Paul tells us that Christ is God's solution to the basic human problem: its separation from God. Unlike the rituals and sacrifices of the high priest in Leviticus 16 that needed to be repeated every year, Jesus' sacrifice needed to take place only once (Hebrews 7:27; 1 Peter 3:18). The writer of the book of Hebrews puts it this way: "Let us then approach the throne of grace with confidence." Furthermore, God's presence, his Holy Spirit, dwells within us. He comforts, teaches, guides, and reminds us what Jesus taught. He is the seal in our hearts that God will complete what he began (Philippians 1:6). In the Spirit, we can hope that one day we will see him just as he is (1 John 3:2) and will be in his presence (Revelation 21:22).

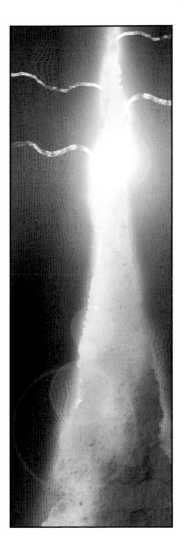

THE MOST HOLY PLACE

The Tabernacle must have been a great mystery for people. Even priests did not know everything about this holy tent. A place where only one man, once a year, entered; where God's powerful presence was visible; where the high priest brought blood and incense to do a ritual of atonement for the sins of the all the people; the Tabernacle was a place of wonder.

The Most Holy Place—or Holy of Holies—was situated at the far end of the Tabernacle. A veil divided the room into two sections. The whole interior of the Tabernacle was dedicated to God as a Holy Place in which only the priests—who God especially chose among all the tribes of the children of Israel— could go. However, this third section was especially set apart, dedicated to God as his unique dwelling place on earth.

The dimensions of the room (see Exodus 26–25) formed a perfect cube of ten cubits—or a cube of about fifteen feet. It contained within it only the ark of the covenant, though some consider the golden altar of incense, which stood directly outside the door in the veil, to be technically a part of the Most Holy Place (Hebrews 9:3–4).

The Most Holy Place functioned as a royal tent. In the Old Testament, God was King. It is no accident then that the Tabernacle, also known as the Tent of Meeting, was placed at the center of Israel's encampment (Numbers 2). It was common practice for the king of any nation to camp at the center of his army as a meeting place for his people. By descending in the cloud, God could live among his people (Exodus 25:8). As king, God provided guidance and protection in this way.

The Most Holy Place also functioned as the center of worship. Archaeologists have discovered buildings with a three-room structure that functioned as temples, just like the Tabernacle. However, only within the Tabernacle did God, the true and only God of the Universe, live. It was the place God chose both as a dwelling place and as a place for meeting with his people.

THE ARK OF THE COVENANT

The ark of the covenant rested in the Most Holy Place; a thick veil separated it from the rest of the Holy Place (Exodus 26:31–33). The ark of the covenant was the place where God met and talked with Moses (Exodus 25:22). The ark was the first item of furniture constructed after God told Moses to build the Tabernacle (Exodus 25:10–22). It was made of acacia wood and covered with gold.

The ark of the covenant was intended to be the central focus of the Most Holy Place in the Tabernacle and later the Temple (Exodus 40:1–21).

Only the high priest could enter the Most Holy Place once a year (Leviticus 16) during *Yom Kippur*, the Day of Atonement. On that day, the high priest would sacrifice and sprinkle blood on the mercy seat—the top of the ark of the covenant where the winged cherubim faced each other—to atone for the sins of the people (Exodus 37:6–9). God set apart the tribe of Levi to carry the ark and stand before him, to serve him, and to bless his name (Deuteronomy 10:8).

THE ARK OF THE COVENANT

Fascinating Facts

- The word ark occurs over 200 times in the Bible. About 30 times, it is in reference to Noah's ark.

- God gave the instructions for building the ark (Exodus 25:8).

- Moses used holy anointing oil to consecrate the ark of the Testimony (Exodus 30:22–26).

- Instructions for moving the ark included covering it with an animal skin, possibly badger, porpoise, or sea cow (Numbers 4:5–6).

- Although the Scripture passages regarding the jar of manna (Exodus 16:33–34) and Aaron's rod (Numbers 17:1–10) do not mention the ark of the covenant, God told Moses to place the jar and the rod before the Testimony (the Tablets of the Law) before the ark was constructed.

- Manna translated means "What is it?"

- The word testimony also occurs later in reference to the ark of the covenant (ark of the Testimony).

- The Tabernacle remained at Shiloh from the time of Joshua 18 to 1 Samuel 4.

- The last location of the ark, mentioned in the Old Testament, is Solomon's Temple (2 Chronicles 35:3).

- In the Temple of Solomon, the carrying poles for the ark stuck out beyond the veil. They could be seen from the Holy Place, but not from outside (1 Kings 8:8).

- Jeremiah predicted that Israel would lose the ark and that they would not even care (Jeremiah 3:16–17).

THE ARK OF THE COVENANT

Contents of the Ark

		OLD TESTAMENT	NEW TESTAMENT	SYMBOLISM
STONE TABLETS WITH TEN COMMANDMENTS		Deuteronomy 10:5	Hebrews 9:4	The stone tablets with the Ten Commandments, written by God's own hand, were to remind the people of God's holy nature (Exodus 10:1–17). Jesus said that he came to fulfill the law (Matthew 5:17–18).
A JAR OF MANNA		Exodus 16:32–34	Hebrews 9:4	The jar of manna reminded the people of God's constant provision (Exodus 16:32–34). Scripture says Christ is the bread of God who comes down from heaven and gives life to the world (John 6:32–35, 48–51).
AARON'S ROD		Numbers 17:10	Hebrews 9:4	Aaron's rod confirmed God's choice and anointing of Aaron as high priest. The Messiah was the chosen and anointed one (Hebrews 3:1, 4:14), just like Aaron (Numbers 17:5).

The references to the ark in Scripture include:

- Ark of testimony
- Ark of the covenant
- Ark of God

Exodus 25:22
Numbers 10:33
1 Samuel 3:3

- Ark of the LORD God
- Holy ark
- Ark of your strength

1 Kings 2:26
2 Chronicles 35:3
Psalm 132:8

The Mercy Seat

God promised to be present upon the mercy seat (Exodus 25:22; see also 30:6, 36). The mercy seat was a kind of portable throne, carried along the poles of the ark and complete with a canopy of angel wings. The cherubim faced the center of the seat while their wings overspread it. The picture of God as King of Israel enthroned on the mercy seat is clear no matter where the ark might be: in the wilderness, in battle, or in his tent (the Tabernacle).

The mercy seat was actually the top or lid of the ark of the covenant measuring 2.5 cubits by 1.5 cubits (3 feet 9 inches by 2 feet 3 inches). It was made of gold and had two golden cherubim at either end.

THE SHEKINAH

Many people think of the cloud in the Most Holy Place as God's *shekinah*. In a late Jewish tradition, the term *shekinah* became associated with God's presence. The word *shekinah* derives from a Hebrew word meaning "dwelling."

The word itself does not appear in the Old Testament. A similar word (*shakan*) occurs in, for example, Exodus 14:20; 40:34–38; Leviticus 9:23, 24; Numbers 14:10; 16:19, 42.

However, in the Exodus and the wilderness experience, God's presence was represented with the cloud during the day and the column of fire during the night.

THE VISIBLE PRESENCE OF GOD

God's presence in the Old Testament was often seen as a fiery glow accompanied by smoke or a cloud.

Genesis 15:17	God is seen in a vision as a smoking fire pot and flaming torch
Exodus 14:24	The LORD is seen as a pillar of fire and cloud
Leviticus 16:2	The LORD appears as a cloud on the mercy seat
Numbers 7:89	The LORD is heard as a voice on the mercy seat
Numbers 9:15–22	The LORD appears over the Tabernacle as a cloud and fire
Deuteronomy 1:33	The LORD leads Israel as fire and cloud
1 Kings 8:10–11	The LORD fills Solomon's temple as a cloud
Isaiah 4:5	Prophecy of God as cloud, smoke and flaming fire
Isaiah 6:4	Isaiah sees God as smoke in the heavenly temple

Christ is God's presence among us. During his earthly ministry, Jesus was Emmanuel—God with us. Now that Jesus has returned to his Father, the Holy Spirit is his presence among us.

The mercy seat was also the ultimate place of appeal for God's grace. It was the place where, once a year, the high priest would sprinkle the blood of sacrifice from the bronze altar. Only on this day, in a precise manner was God to be approached in the Most Holy Place, and only by the chosen high priest. Today, because Jesus our Great High Priest has made once for all time his sacrifice, we are urged as believers to "boldly approach the throne of grace…" (Hebrews 4:16).

Jesus and the Pillar

From the moment the Israelites left Egypt, danger followed them all the way. Between the Egyptian army pursuing them and the dangers in the wilderness, the Israelites were a crowd of scared, tired people. They had seen God's power in Egypt, but they were walking into the unknown. Seeing the cloud during the day and the column of fire during the night was probably a great comfort. The pillar of cloud and fire functioned as a reminder of God's guiding and protective care, shown in Exodus 14:19, the pillar interposed between Israel and the pursuing Egyptian army, striking fear into the camp of Egypt and encouraging the Israelites.

When Jesus gathered his disciples for a last conversation, he told them about his departure from them. Fear, anxiety, and uncertainty grew in their hearts. However, Jesus left them with a great promise: the Comforter would come in his place. The Holy Spirit would come to each of Jesus' disciples to bring comfort, to teach, and to guide. Acts 2:1–4 narrates the coming of the Spirit. It describes a *theophany* (see sidebar): the sound of a "violent wind" and "what seemed to be tongues of fire." Any reader familiar with God's appearances in the Old Testament would recognize these descriptions as a theophany. Just like the cloud and the pillar of fire, the Holy Spirit continues God's guiding care for his people.

THEOPHANY

The word *theophany* derives from a Greek word meaning "appearance of God." A theophany is another instance of God's special presence.

In some theophanies, God appears in human form, as when he appeared to Abraham near the great trees of Mamre (Genesis 18).

In other occasions, God appears with a great display of power. His appearance at Mount Sinai filled the Israelites with great fear (Exodus 19:16; see also Nahum 1:2–6).

However, God can also appear in a quiet, gentle way, as he did to Elijah at Horeb (1 Kings 19).

Paul's vision of the resurrected Christ was a theophanic revelation (Acts 9:1–6).

MANIFESTATIONS OF GOD'S PRESENCE

Text	Setting	Manifestation
Genesis 15:12–21	God met Abraham and made a covenant with him. This covenant sealed God's promise to give to Abraham a land.	God's presence occurred in the form of darkness and fire.
Exodus 13:21–22	As the children of Israel were leaving, God guided them away from Egypt.	God's presence appeared as a cloud during the day and a column of fire during the night.
Exodus 19:16–20; 24:16–17	After three months out of Egypt, the people of Israel arrived at the foot of Mount Sinai.	God's presence became visible with a great display of power. Darkness, thunder, and lightening covered the mountain.
Exodus 40:36–38; Numbers 9:15–23;	The Israelites camped around the Tabernacle. God would let them know when to move or remain in place.	God's presence took the form of the cloud over and inside the Tabernacle. When God decided it was time to move, the cloud lifted.

The Journey of the Ark

1. Exodus 25—God gives Moses directions to build the ark of the covenant.
2. Exodus 26:31–33—The veil is woven.
3. Exodus 40:1–21—The ark in the Tabernacle.
4. Leviticus 16; Numbers 4, 10, 14; Deuteronomy 10—The ark is carried for 40 years in wilderness.

Exodus 16:33–34—Manna laid before the Testimony.

Numbers 17:8, 10—Aaron's rod laid before the Testimony.

5. Joshua 3—Priests carry the ark across the Jordan River.

8. Joshua 8—After conquering the town of Ai, the covenant was remembered at Mt. Ebal.

7. Joshua 6—The ark is carried around Jericho.

6. Joshua 4—People build a memorial after the Jordan River parts.

9. Joshua 18:1—Tabernacle at Shiloh.

10. Judges 20:27—Ark taken to Bethel.

13. 1 Samuel 6—The Philistines return the ark to Beth Shemesh.

11. 1 Samuel 1:3, 3:3—The LORD speaks to the child Samuel who is sleeping near the ark at Shiloh.

14. 1 Samuel 6:19–21—Men struck dead by the LORD for looking into the ark.

12. 1 Samuel 4—Philistines take the ark of God.

15. 1 Samuel 7—Ark brought to the house of Abinadab in Kiriath Jearim. It stays there 20 years.

16. 1 Samuel 14:18—Saul brings the ark to war camp temporarily.

17. 2 Samuel 6—Ark moved on a cart to the house of Obed-Edom for three months. Uzzah is struck dead.

19. 2 Samuel 15—David flees Jerusalem with the ark but sends it back to Jerusalem.

18. 2 Samuel 6:12–17—David brings the ark to Jerusalem and places it in a tent that is set up for it.

20. 1 Kings 8—Solomon has ark brought into Most Holy Place in the Temple.

21. 2 Chronicles 34:14–35:3—Josiah recovers book of the Law and puts ark in Temple.

Scholars believe that when the Babylonians destroyed Jerusalem (586 BC), and plundered the Temple, the ark was probably taken by Nebuchadnezzar and destroyed.

22. Jeremiah 3:16,17—Prophecy of Jeremiah that the ark would not be thought of or missed nor will another be made. It will be replaced by the LORD'S presence.

Hebrews 9:11–12—When Christ came as high priest of the good things that are already here, he went through the greater and more perfect Tabernacle that is not man-made, that is to say, not a part of this creation. He did not enter by means of the blood of goats and calves; but he entered the Most Holy Place once for all by his own blood, having obtained eternal redemption.

Revelation 11:19—Then God's temple in heaven was opened, and within his temple was seen the ark of his covenant. And there came flashes of lightning, rumblings, peals of thunder, an earthquake and a great hailstorm.

Jesus and the Ark of the Covenant

SHADOW (TYPE)		OLD TESTAMENT	NEW TESTAMENT	BIBLE REFERENCES
THE TABERNACLE		The place where God as spirit dwelled among his people.	Jesus is God in the flesh dwelling among his people.	Exodus 25; Isaiah 9:6 Matthew 1:22–23 John 1:14, 14:8–10
THE HIGH PRIEST		The high priest offered gifts and sacrifices for sins in the Most Holy Place.	Jesus is our high priest of the true Tabernacle made by God, not by man.	Exodus 28:1; 29:9; Leviticus 16:30 Hebrews 4:14–15; 8:1–3; 9:11
THE SACRIFICE		Each year, the high priest offered a blood sacrifice for the sin of the people.	Jesus was the perfect and final sacrifice for all time.	Exodus 30:10 Romans 3:21–26; 5:8–10 Hebrews 9:12–15; 10:1–14
THE ARK		Place of God's presence.	Jesus is God in human form.	Exodus 25:22 John 1:14
ARK CONTENTS: TABLE OF THE LAW		The Law given by God.	Jesus said that he came to "fulfill the Law."	Exodus 20:1–17 Matthew 5:17–18; 22:36–40 Luke 16:16–17
ARK CONTENTS: AARON'S ROD		Represented God's choice.	Jesus is God's choice.	Numbers 17:5, 8, 10 Matthew 3:17 Hebrews 3:1–2; 9:4
ARK CONTENTS: MANNA		Given by God as food to the people in the wilderness.	Jesus called himself the "bread of life."	Exodus 16 John 6:35, 48–51

THE ARK IN BATTLE

When God brought the children of Israel out of Egypt, Pharaoh and his armies chased them. The Israelites were afraid and complained to God. Moses said to them, "Do not be afraid… The LORD will fight for you…" (Exodus 14:13–14).

A. K. Abhirama

The other nations of the ancient Middle East also thought their gods were warriors. In fact, one of the chief gods of the Canaanites, the inhabitants of the land God promised to Abraham, was a warrior god: Baal. At the time, the Canaanites and all the peoples around them believed that it was the strength of their gods that gave them political and territorial power. When God took his people out of Egypt and gave the land to the Israelites, it was a powerful statement about who God is: the only, true, and mighty God.

The liberation of Israel from Egypt was, in fact, a confrontation between the LORD, the God of the universe, and Pharaoh, himself a false god, and the gods of Egypt. The ten plagues had the purpose that Pharaoh, and the Israelites themselves, would "know that there is no one like me in all the earth" (Exodus 9:14).

The ark of the covenant was the visual representation of God's presence. For this reason, it travelled ahead of the Israelite army on their way to the Promised Land. In fact, when Israel finally travelled to the West of the Jordan river, God crossed the river first. The Levites carrying the

Today the ark is not necessary because God's presence travels with each and every believer. Before going away, Jesus promised that he would be with his church forever, and he also promised to send the Holy Spirit. The Holy Spirit is God's presence in our midst.

ark of the covenant walked through dry ground. As the Israelites crossed, the priests raised some commemorative stones to remember God's passing through the river. God, the great King, was ahead of his army.

RAMESSES II'S MILITARY CAMP AT KADESH

Ramesses II's military camp. In James H. Breasted, *The Battle of Kadesh* (Chicago: University of Chicago, 1903), pl. 1.

The image above shows a representation of Ramesses II's military camp at Kadesh. Ramesses II traveled north—to what is now Syria—to fight against the powerful king of Hatti, Muwatalli.

The relief shows Ramesses II's tent, with an exterior court, an inner reception chamber, and the innermost room, the throne room. The three-section structure of Ramesses II's tent suggests important similarities with the Tabernacle that God commanded Moses to make.

Like a king fighting in the midst of his armies, God dwelt in the midst of his armies.

The Bible narrates two contrasting times when the ark was taken to battle. The first time, God ordered it; the second, he did not. On the first occasion, God instructed Joshua to have the priests take the ark into battle around Jericho (Joshua 6:6–20). The priests encircled the city for a week, with the ark and the armies. Because the Israelites obeyed God's orders, God granted victory in battle to the Israelites.

The second incident of the ark in battle is in 1 Samuel 4:3–22. The leaders of Israel took the ark into battle with them without asking God. The results were disastrous: the Philistine army defeated Israel and captured the ark. At the end, because of God's intervention, the Philistines returned the ark to Israel (1 Samuel 6).

Because God's presence was in the ark of the covenant, treating it like a magic amulet, like an object to use when necessary, was a great offense and a breaking of the third commandment. Having the ark in their midst was a confirmation of God's faithfulness to his promises: he promised he would be with them and fight along with and for them.

WHERE IS THE ARK TODAY?

The Old Testament mentions the ark for the last time in 2 Chronicles 35:3. There, after finding the book of the law, King Josiah celebrated the Passover. He then instructed the Levites to return the ark to the Temple. The New Testament only mentions the ark in two places: John 1:14 (an allusion) and Hebrews 8:2, 5; 9:1-24. Yet, these are references to the Old Testament sacred object.

- The probability is that the ark was destroyed in 586 BC when Nebuchadnezzar captured Jerusalem. There is no mention of it in the list of temple treasures that the Babylonian King took (2 Kings 25:13–17). When the exiles later returned to Jerusalem to rebuild the Temple, they were allowed to bring several thousand articles from the temple with them. However, there is no mention of the ark (Ezra 1:7–11).

- When the Roman general Pompey conquered Jerusalem and entered the Most Holy Place in the Temple, he famously affirmed that he had seen nothing but "an empty and mysterious space." Although for Pompey the expression was in reference to images of God, it implies that the ark was absent as well.

- Over the centuries there have been claims that the ark survived the Babylonian invasion. In 2 Maccabees 2:4–8 the prophet Jeremiah is said to have hidden the ark in a cave on Mt. Nebo, which is east of the Dead Sea in today's Jordan.

- An Ethiopian legend has Menelik, King Solomon's son by the Queen of Sheba, carrying the ark to Ethiopia (a copy of the ark was left behind in Jerusalem). The ark is alleged to be hidden in a church in the city of Axum, where it has been protected by generations of guardian monks.

- Fueled by the popularity of the movie *Raiders of the Lost Ark*, recent years have seen numerous searches and appeals for money to fund the recovery of the ark. A cave near the Dead Sea, or in one of the tunnels under Jerusalem's Temple Mount, are only two of the suggested locations. Claims of having found the ark have never been accompanied by any pictures or other evidence.

Section 3

LIVING WITH GOD IN THE WILDERNESS

The Wilderness

The wilderness played an important role, affecting life in ancient Israel in several different ways. For instance, every year, at the beginning and end of summer, a hot, dry desert wind blows from the east. This wind, called *sirocco*, raises the temperature and can be quite destructive to vegetation. The wind was a yearly reminder to Israel that the wilderness was within reach.

The wilderness also became a powerful symbol in the Scriptures. The symbols were apparently contradictory: negative, on one hand, and positive, on the other. First, wilderness was a place of danger where only wild beasts lived. It was a place of death and barrenness. God is life, fruitfulness, light, order, and harmony; in contrast, the wilderness was a place of death, barrenness, darkness, and chaos.

However, the wilderness also was a place of transition, a place for meeting God. The wilderness experience began after the Israelites came out of Egypt, on their way to the Promised Land. The wilderness represented the transition from being different tribes and from being slaves for generations, to becoming a holy nation, a worshiping people,

God's treasured possession. The wilderness journey was a time of preparation. Although God promised to be with them and fight for them, the people needed to learn how to trust God. Trust requires time to grow. In addition, the trust that holds firmly is usually born in times of difficulties. True worship and faith arise from a heart grateful to God for his love, grace, and mercy.

The presence of God in the midst of the camp could not have contrasted more than it did in the wilderness. God intended the Israelite camp to be an oasis of life, grace, and light. Like Noah's ark in the midst of the flood, it was meant to be a place of life in the midst of death, a place of order and harmony in the midst of disorder and chaos.

In this place of contrasts, God taught the tribes of Israel to be a holy nation, a kingdom of priests. He taught them how to be God's people.

THE SONG OF MOSES (EXODUS 15:1–18)

Having crossed the Red Sea, still terrified by God's miraculous victory over Pharaoh and his armies, the Israelites stood at the edge of the powerful sea. Tired, still scared, and amazed by what God had done, the people exploded in spontaneous singing. Their song celebrated God's spectacular victory, giving God the deserved praise. The song presents God as warrior—the Divine Warrior—who fought for his people and defeated the enemy. Verses 11 and 12 are the heart of the song, confirming the purpose God repeated: "and the Egyptians will know that I am the LORD..." (Exodus 14:4, 18).

The Israelites also asked in the song, "Who among the gods is like you, O LORD?" His power and grace shone in more than just his victory. His unfailing love—the love that is born from a deep commitment—moved God to free the children of Israel and defeat their enemies. God remembered "his covenant with Abraham, with Isaac and with Jacob" (Exodus 2:24), and his deep, committed love for them moved him to act. The same love moved God to guide his people through the wilderness to the place where he would make a covenant with them. His victory was a testimony for the Israelites that the LORD is the true God. It also was a testimony to the nations that Israel's God is the true God. The song ends with the only possible conclusion: "The LORD will reign forever and ever" (Exodus 15:18).

THE RED SEA

Although it is common knowledge that Israel crossed the "Red Sea," it is not completely clear that the Bible says that. "Red Sea" was the translation used in the King James Bible. The Hebrew expression, *yam suph*, probably means "Sea of Reeds." The Hebrew word for sea, *yam*, is used for any large body of water—such as a lake, a river, the sea. Far more important, the word *suph* appears to mean "reed." So, what sea did Moses lead the children of Israel through? The precise location of the crossing of this sea depends on the route for the Exodus, on the length of traveling that a large group of people could do, and on the knowledge of location of biblical places mentioned in Exodus:

- The traditional place for the crossing is the north end of the Gulf of Suez, which is part of the Red Sea.

- Lake Sibronis and Lake Menzaleh are located near the Mediterranean Sea.

- Lake Ballah, Lake Timsah, the Great Bitter Lakes, or the Little Bitter Lakes, north of the Gulf of Suez and west of the Wilderness of Shur.

Because of our inadequate knowledge of the places the Bible mentions in Exodus, we cannot be sure where the crossing of the sea occurred. Not knowing the precise place, however, does not mean that the event did not occur, or that it was not as miraculous as the Bible describes it.

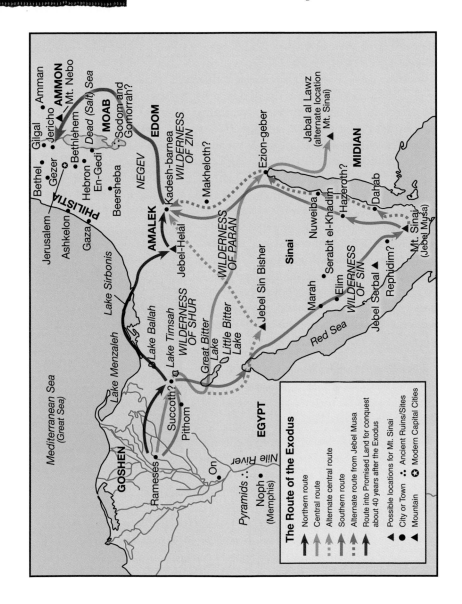

The Route of the Exodus

EXODUS 15:1–18

Then Moses and the Israelites sang this song to the LORD: "I will sing to the LORD, for he is highly exalted. The horse and its rider he has hurled into the sea. The LORD is my strength and my song; he has become my salvation. He is my God, and I will praise him, my father's God, and I will exalt him. The LORD is a warrior; the Lord is his name. Pharaoh's chariots and his army he has hurled into the sea. The best of Pharaoh's officers are drowned in the Red Sea. The deep waters have covered them; they sank to the depths like a stone. "Your right hand, O LORD, was majestic in power. Your right hand, O LORD, shattered the enemy. In the greatness of your majesty you threw down those who opposed you. You unleashed your burning anger; it consumed them like stubble.

By the blast of your nostrils the waters piled up. The surging waters stood firm like a wall; the deep waters congealed in the heart of the sea. "The enemy boasted, 'I will pursue, I will overtake them. I will divide the spoils; I will gorge myself on them. I will draw my sword and my hand will destroy them.' But you blew with your breath, and the sea covered them. They sank like lead in the mighty waters.

"Who among the gods is like you, O LORD? Who is like you—majestic in holiness, awesome in glory, working wonders? You stretched out your right hand and the earth swallowed them.

"In your unfailing love you will lead the people you have redeemed. In your strength you will guide them to your holy dwelling. The nations will hear and

Moses   Michelangelo

tremble; anguish will grip the people of Philistia. The chiefs of Edom will be terrified, the leaders of Moab will be seized with trembling, the people of Canaan will melt away; terror and dread will fall upon them. By the power of your arm they will be as still as a stone—until your people pass by, O LORD, until the people you bought pass by. You will bring them in and plant them on the mountain of your inheritance—the place, O LORD, you made for your dwelling, the sanctuary, O LORD, your hands established. The LORD will reign for ever and ever."

ISRAEL AT SINAI

Exodus 19 describes Israel arriving at Sinai. This chapter is important for understanding the events at Sinai, where Israel spent over two years (Numbers 10:11). God addressed the people as "the house of Jacob… the people of Israel…" (Exodus 19:3) as a way to remind them that they were the people of the covenant, the descendants of Abraham. What was about to happen at Sinai was not a new covenant with the people but an extension of the covenant God made with Abraham. All of the events before and after this moment at the foot of the mountain assume that God is the Creator. The whole earth belongs to him, yet he made Israel his "treasured possession" (19:5). The LORD would not be the God of the priests, or the king alone, but the God of Israel. The whole nation would become "a kingdom of priests and a holy nation" (19:6).

A powerful manifestation of God, a theophany, dominates this passage. God does not always appear in such a fearsome manner. In fact, in 1 Kings 19:11–13, the LORD appeared to Elijah in a gentle way. Yet, in Exodus 19, the powerful theophany had a purpose: "so that the people will hear me speaking with you and will always put their trust in you" (19:9). God was validating Moses'

leadership. The theophany produced a state of awe, almost like terror (19:16). Although the Israelites were in a covenant relationship, one in which God treated Abraham as a friend (Isaiah 41:8 and James 2:23), God made it clear to them that the LORD was God and they were his creatures. In this context of his power and authority, God revealed to the Israelites the Ten Commandments. The commandments were the way for people to live in this covenant relationship with God. It was what made it possible for sinful people to live with a holy, powerful God in their midst.

Domenico Beccafumi

EXODUS 19:1–6

In the third month after the Israelites left Egypt—on the very day—they came to the Desert of Sinai. After they set out from Rephidim, they entered the Desert of Sinai, and Israel camped there in the desert in front of the mountain.

Then Moses went up to God, and the Lord called to him from the mountain and said, "This is what you are to say to the house of Jacob and what you are to tell the people of Israel: 'You yourselves have seen what I did to Egypt, and how I carried you on eagles' wings and brought you to myself. Now if you obey me fully and keep my covenant, then out of all nations you will be my treasured possession. Although the whole earth is mine, you will be for me a kingdom of priests and a holy nation.' These are the words you are to speak to the Israelites."

THE TEN COMMANDMENTS

I am the LORD your God who brought you out of Egypt
out of the land of slavery.

1 You shall have no other gods before me.

2 You shall not make for yourself an idol in the
form of anything in heaven above or on the earth
beneath or in the waters below.

3 You shall not misuse the name of the LORD your God.

4 Remember the Sabbath day by keeping it holy.

5 Honor your father and your mother, so that you may
live long in the land the LORD your God is giving you.

6 You shall not murder.

7 You shall not commit adultery.

8 You shall not steal.

9 You shall not give false testimony against your neighbor.

10 You shall not covet your neighbor's house…
or anything that belongs to your neighbor.

EXODUS 20:1-17 *NIV*

The Arrangement of the Camp

The Israelite camp in the wilderness was not a regular nomadic camp. The book of Numbers describes the organization of a military camp. Israel became God's army, and God, Israel's king, went along with them in the military march. The organization of the tribes depended on military strength: Judah had the most warriors of all the tribes, so they guarded the east side of the Tabernacle. The east in the ancient world was an important, symbolic point of reference. The Tabernacle, like the Temple in Jerusalem, always faced east.

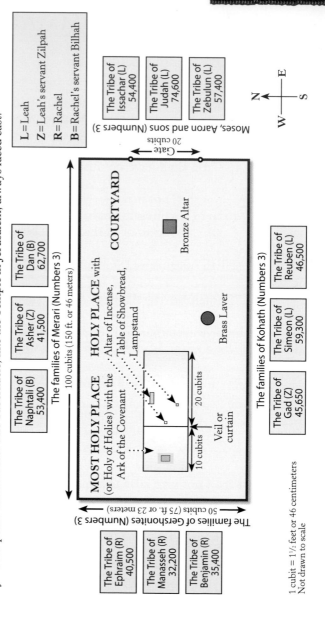

L = Leah
Z = Leah's servant Zilpah
R = Rachel
B = Rachel's servant Bilhah

The Tribe of Issachar (L) 54,400
The Tribe of Judah (L) 74,600
The Tribe of Zebulun (L) 57,400

Moses, Aaron and sons (Numbers 3)

Gate 20 cubits

COURTYARD

Bronze Altar

The Tribe of Naphtali (B) 53,400
The Tribe of Asher (Z) 41,500
The Tribe of Dan (B) 62,700

The families of Merari (Numbers 3)

100 cubits (150 ft. or 46 meters)

HOLY PLACE with
Altar of Incense,
Table of Showbread,
Lampstand

MOST HOLY PLACE
(or Holy of Holies) with the
Ark of the Covenant

Brass Laver

20 cubits

Veil or curtain

10 cubits

The families of Kohath (Numbers 3)

The Tribe of Gad (Z) 45,650
The Tribe of Simeon (L) 59,300
The Tribe of Reuben (L) 46,500

The families of Gershonites (Numbers 3)

50 cubits (75 ft. or 23 meters)

The Tribe of Ephraim (R) 40,500
The Tribe of Manasseh (R) 32,200
The Tribe of Benjamin (R) 35,400

1 cubit = 1½ feet or 46 centimeters
Not drawn to scale

N W E S

136

ARRANGEMENT OF THE MARCH

NUMBERS 10:11

On the twentieth day of the second month of the second year, the cloud lifted from above the tabernacle of the Testimony...

As the tribes of Israel traveled through the wilderness toward the promised land, they formed a military march. At the head, God's presence led the contingent, as the Levites carried the ark. The tribes followed according to their military strength.

NUMBERS 10:35-36

Whenever the ark set out, Moses said,

"Rise up, O Lord!

May your enemies be scattered;

may your foes flee before you."

Whenever it came to rest, he said,

"Return, O Lord,

to the countless thousands of Israel."

| L = Leah |
| Z = Leah's servant Zilpah |
| R = Rachel |
| B = Rachel's servant Bilhah |

The Tribe of Dan (B)	The Tribe of Ephraim (R)		The Tribe of Reuben (L)		The Tribe of Issachar (L)	
The Tribe of Asher (Z)	The Tribe of Manasseh (R)	Levites carry sacred objects	The Tribe of Simeon (L)	Levites carry Tabernacle	The Tribe of Judah (L)	Levites carry ark of the covenant
The Tribe of Naphtali (B)	The Tribe of Benjamin (R)		The Tribe of Gad (Z)		The Tribe of Zebulun (L)	

137

ORGANIZATION OF TRIBES, CAMP AND MARCH

God rescued the children of Israel so that they would worship him and to fulfill what he had promised to Abraham: give them a land flowing with milk and honey. To do that, God organized the tribes into a people; a worshiping people and God's own army. The different ways in which the tribes are organized show two interests: their order of importance and their location in the camp or the march. Both display their place in God's plan of redemption for Israel and for the whole world.

1. The first column shows a *chronological* order of birth of Jacob's sons.

2. The second column shows another birth order based on Jacob's four wives. Leah, the most prolific of the wives, takes prominence. Rachel follows her, and the two maidservants, Bilhah and Zilpah, come at the end, in order of importance.

3. The third column shows the order in which Jacob blessed his sons before his own death. Leah's sons received his blessings first, speaking of their importance in the story of Genesis. Rachel's sons receive their father's blessings at the end. The children of both wives, then, surround the children of maidservants Bilhah and Zilpah. And, further, Bilhah's children surround Zilpah's children.

4. The census in Numbers 1 grouped them according to the order each tribe would have in the camp around the Tabernacle. The census was not one of population; it was a military census: "…all the men in Israel twenty years old or more who are able to serve in the army" (Numbers 1:3).

5. This order was further clarified in Numbers 2, in which the tribes are organized in geographical terms. The East played a prominent role in the life of the cultures of the ancient Near East. Because Judah was the strongest tribe in military terms, it occupied the East side, right in front of the Tabernacle. Judah, not Reuben—the oldest son—had the place of honor.

1 Birth Order Genesis 30–31	2 Birth Order Genesis 35:22	3 Order of Blessing Genesis 49	4 Order of Census Numbers 1:20–42	5 Order of the Camp Numbers 2:1–34	6 Order of the March Numbers 10:11–33
					Levites—L ark
Reuben—L	Reuben—L	Reuben—L	Reuben—L	(E) Judah—L	Judah—L
Simeon—L	Simeon—L	Simeon—L	Simeon—L	(E) Issachar—L	Issachar—L
Levi—L	Levi—L	Levi—L	Gad—Z	(E) Zebulun—L	Zebulun—L
Judah—L	Judah—L	Judah—L	Judah—L	(S) Reuben—L	Levites—L Tabernacle
Dan—B	Issachar—L	Zebulun—L	Issachar—L	(S) Simeon—L	Reuben—L
Naphtali—B	Zebulun—L	Issachar—L	Zebulun—L	(S) Gad—Z	Simeon—L
Gad—Z	Joseph—R	Dan—B	Ephraim—(R)	(Middle) Levites—L	Gad—Z
Asher—Z	Benjamin—R	Gad—Z	Manasseh—(R)	(W) Ephraim—R	Levites—L Holy Things
Issachar—L	Dan—B	Asher—Z	Benjamin—R	(W) Manasseh—R	Ephraim—R
Zebulun—L	Naphtali—B	Naphtali—B	Dan—B	(W) Benjamin—R	Manasseh—R
Joseph—R	Gad—Z	Joseph—R	Asher—Z	(N) Dan—B	Benjamin—R
Benjamin—R	Asher—Z	Benjamin—R	Naphtali—B	(N) Asher—Z	Dan—B
				(N) Naphtali—B	Asher—Z
					Naphtali—B

L = Leah	**(E)** = East
Z = Leah's servant Zilpah	**(S)** = South
R = Rachel	**(W)** = West
B = Rachel's servant Bilhah	**(N)** = North

The Feasts

A WORSHIPING COMMUNITY

An important part of being God's people consisted in knowing how to give God proper worship. God is more than a king who requires loyalty and dedication. He is the God of creation, the only one worthy of worship and adoration.

When God freed Israel from Egypt, he made his purposes clear:

To show that he alone is the true and mighty God, Creator of heaven and earth.

To make Israel's children his own people, his treasured possession.

To have a people that worshiped him as the true and only God.

To keep his promise to Abraham to make his descendants great and many, and to give them a land "flowing with milk and honey."

The children of Israel were a worshiping people. In the wilderness, Israel came to understand God's centrality. God was at the center of the camp, and his presence affected all of life. The children of Israel organized their lives around God's presence: their movements, their feasts, and their daily routine. A large section of the Pentateuch—the first five books of the Bible—deals with matters of worship: rituals, sacrifices, prayers, and purity. Israel's worship is most clear in the Psalms.

The people's worship was a recognition of their total dependence on God. Their life in the wilderness was a life of faith—faith that God would provide food and water, security from the dangers of the wilderness.

EXODUS 15:20,21
Then Miriam the prophetess, Aaron's sister, took a tambourine in her hand, and all the women followed her, with tambourines and dancing.

Miriam sang to them: "Sing to the Lord, for he is highly exalted. The horse and its rider he has hurled into the sea."

THE CALENDAR

God established the feasts and holy days of the Bible to remind the people of the great things he had done for them: miracles, victories, and provision. These special days were organized in Leviticus 23. God appointed seven holidays for the people as times to meet with him. Just as God had organized the space of the camp in the wilderness, he organized the time into *sacred*—time dedicated to God alone—and *common*—when the people could do their work, traveling, entertainment, and so on. Although most of the feasts originated in the wilderness around the Tabernacle, some other holidays developed later.

The purposes of the feasts were:

- To be a reminder
- To rest (sabbath)
- To give thanks through offerings
- To repent and offer sacrifices
- To read the Scriptures

As the first Passover was about to happen in Exodus 12, God also established the order of the months. This was the first Jewish calendar used to determine the holidays (religious year). The Gregorian calendar used by most Western nations today is a solar calendar. The Jewish calendar uses both lunar and solar movements. The months are determined by the moon; the year by the sun.

Following the Babylonian exile in the sixth century BC, the Jewish calendar reflected the Babylonian names of the months. These names still exist today in the current Jewish religious calendar.

Today this religious calendar is only used by observant Jews. Most people in Israel use the Gregorian calendar.

Feasts of the Bible Calendar

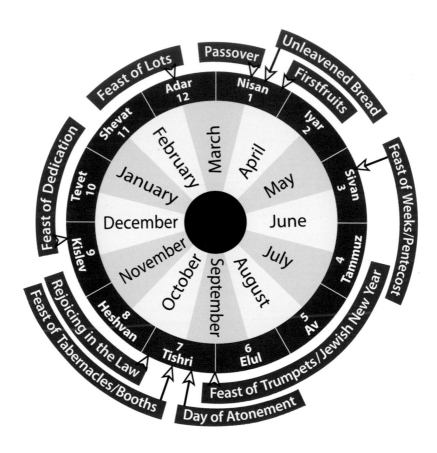

PASSOVER

In Exodus 12, God gave Moses the instructions and requirements for the Passover.

EXODUS 12	CHRIST
12:1–2—The feast marked a new year, a new beginning for the Israelites.	In Christ, every believer is a new creation (2 Corinthians 5:17). Old things and the old life are past.
12:5—A male lamb in its first year was taken into the home on the tenth of *Nisan* (the first month of the Jewish calendar). While in the home, it was closely inspected to see if there were any blemishes or disfigurements. If it was without defect, it was then sacrificed on the fourteenth of *Nisan*.	Christ was closely inspected by: • Pilate (Matthew 27:11–26; Luke 23:1–6; 13–25; John 18:28–19:16) • Herod (Luke 23:8–12) • Annas (John 18:12–13; 19–24) • Caiaphas (Matthew 26:57). They could find no fault in him. Christ is the "lamb without blemish or defect" (1 Peter 1:19).
12:6—The "whole community" of God's people was required to participate in the sacrifice.	Accepting Christ's sacrifice is required for all who want to be part of God's community (Romans 3:21–26).
12:7, 12, 22—The blood of the sacrificed lamb was applied to the door frame—the lintel and side posts. Because of the covering of blood, the house was spared from God's plague.	Christ shed his blood to rescue his people. We need to be covered or justified by the blood of the Lamb to be rescued from condemnation (Romans 3:25; 5:9). Christ is the Lamb that takes away the sins of the world (John 1:29).
12:14—The Passover was to be kept as a remembrance forever.	During the Last Supper, Jesus refers to the bread as "my body given for you; do this in remembrance of me" (Luke 22:19).
12:46—God commanded Israel not to break any bones of the sacrificed lamb.	To speed up Jesus' death, the Roman soldiers were going to break his legs. However, Jesus was already dead, so his bones remained unbroken (John 19:32–33).

The Passover is the Old Testament feast that celebrates and remembers God's liberation of Israel from Egypt. After Joseph saved Egypt from starvation (Genesis 41), the Israelites lived in Egypt as guests. Eventually, the Egyptians forgot about Joseph and enslaved the Israelites (Exodus 1:6–14). The book of Exodus explains how God freed his people from Egypt. Because of the hardness of Pharaoh's heart, God punished Egypt with ten plagues (Exodus 7–11). During the last plague, God killed all the first-born—humans and animals—in the land of Egypt. However, God gave his people a way to escape the destruction: a lamb could take the place of the first-born in the family. God gave Moses the instructions for the time when God's punishment passed over the Israelite homes (Exodus 12). This is the Passover. The Passover feast was to be repeated throughout the generations as a memorial forever. The following section compares the Passover *seder*—meaning *order*—with the New Testament description of the Lord's Supper.

First Cup and Kiddush ("sanctification")

Seder Before the *Seder* began, traditionally a woman lit special candles to mark the commencement of this sacred time. Immediately after this, the head of the table raised the first cup of wine—the cup of sanctification—and blessed it.

Lord's Supper According to Luke 22:17–18, "After taking the cup, he gave thanks and said, 'Take this and divide it among you. For I tell you I will not drink again of the fruit of the vine until the kingdom of God comes.'"

The First Washing of the Hands and the Bitter Herbs

Seder As everyone got ready to partake of the Passover meal, the leader of the Passover washed his hands. Then a plate with salted water was passed around into which

everyone dipped a piece of lettuce or parsley (*karpas*). The salt was a reminder of the tears the Israelites shed during their bondage in Egypt. The green herb was a reminder of a new beginning.

LORD'S SUPPER Jesus went further than the traditional hand washing and taught his disciples humility by washing their feet (John 13:1–17). During the remembrance of the Israelites' tears, Judas' betrayal was likely also a bitter experience for Jesus (Mark 14:20).

THE AFIKOMEN

SEDER The leader took three *matzo* breads and placed them in a special bag with three compartments. The middle *matzah* was broken and one piece placed back in the *matzo* bag. The other piece was hidden under a pillow and was called *Afikomen*.

LORD'S SUPPER Although the practice of the *Afikomen* goes back to antiquity, it is quite possible that it originated after the Romans destroyed the Second Temple in AD 70. In other words, it probably was not practiced in Jesus' time.

THE SECOND CUP AND THE HAGGADAH

SEDER The leader took the second cup of wine (the cup of plagues) and blessed it. No one drank from it until the *Haggadah* ("the telling") was finished. At this point a child asked a series of questions and the leader of the ceremony would tell the story of God's redemption in the Exodus. Traditionally, the answer had to cover at least three elements of the Passover celebration: (1) The Passover sacrifice, (2) the bitter herbs, and (3) the unleavened bread (*matzo*).

LORD'S SUPPER In the Gospel account of the Lord's Supper, the words, "This is my body…" are Jesus' re-interpretation of the Passover. It is here that the sacrificed lamb and the unleavened bread receive greater meaning: Jesus is the Lamb of God (John 1:29) sacrificed in our place (1 Peter 1:17–21) and he is the Bread of Life that comes down from heaven (John 6: 33-35).

FIRST PART OF THE HALLEL AND THE SECOND CUP

SEDER At the end of the *Haggadah*, the leader raised the second cup of wine and invited all to sing the first part of the *Hallel*, which is the recitation of Psalms 113 and 114. Then everyone drank the second cup, the cup of plagues.

LORD'S SUPPER The New Testament does not give a detailed account of Jesus' last actions, but rather focuses on the New Covenant (1 Cor. 11:25) and Jesus' sacrifice about to occur. Although they might have recited the first part of the *Hallel* and taken the second cup, it is not registered in the Scriptures.

SECOND HAND WASHING AND PASSOVER MEAL

SEDER All washed their hands. Then the leader took the *matzo* breads and broke them into pieces.

Based on Exodus 6:6–7, Jewish tradition has incorporated four cups of wine into the Passover celebration. "Therefore, say to the Israelites: 'I am the LORD, and I will bring you out from under the yoke of the Egyptians. I will free you from being slaves to them, and I will redeem you with an outstretched arm and with mighty acts of judgment. I will take you as my own people…'"

The Cup of **SANCTIFICATION**	"… I will *bring you*…"
The Cup of **PLAGUES**	"…I will *free you*…"
The Cup of **REDEMPTION**	"… I will *redeem you*…"
The Cup of **PRAISE** (also called Cup of Acceptance)	"… I will *take you*…"

The leader dipped the bread into a mixture of bitter herbs and distributed them to the participants. The meal was then taken.

LORD'S SUPPER As was traditional in the celebration of the Passover, Jesus dipped a piece of bread; however, he used this moment to indicate who his betrayer would be (John 13:26).

THE GRACE AFTER MEALS AND THE THIRD CUP

SEDER When the meal was finished, no one ate any other food. Instead, the leader of the celebration poured a third cup of wine. Everyone offered another blessing on the third cup of wine, called the cup of redemption, and drank from this cup.

LORD'S SUPPER After the meal, Jesus got up, took a *matzah* bread, and said, "This is my body given for you; do this in remembrance of me" (Luke 22:19). Then he continued with the third cup. He blessed it and said, "This is the cup of the new covenant in my blood; do this, whenever you drink it, in remembrance of me" (1 Corinthians 11:25).

THE SECOND PART OF THE HALLEL AND THE FOURTH CUP

SEDER Once everyone drank the third cup, they recited the second part of the *Hallel* (praise), which consists of Psalms 115–118. No one drank wine between the third cup and the end of the second part of the *Hallel*. At the end of the singing, they drank the fourth cup of wine, called the cup of praise. Then the *Seder* ended.

LORD'S SUPPER Jesus and the disciples finished the Lord's Supper, and Matthew tells us, "When they had sung a hymn, they went out to the Mount of Olives" (Matthew 26:30). The hymn was probably the *Hallel*. The fourth cup was not drunk! "I tell you, I will not drink of this fruit of the vine from now on until that day when I drink it anew with you in my Father's kingdom" (Matthew 26:29). The last cup of the Passover will be drunk at the wedding feast of the Lamb (Revelation 19:9).

THE OLD TESTAMENT PASSOVER

The Passover was a celebration, remembrance, thanksgiving and participation in God's mighty acts of salvation for his people. The New Testament equivalent of the Passover, the Lord's Supper, functions in similar ways for Christians today.

1. The Lord's Supper is a time of remembrance and thanksgiving (Luke 22:19; 1 Corinthians 11:24–25).

2. The Lord's Supper is a time for refreshing and communion (Romans 5:10; 1 Corinthians 10:16).

3. The Lord's Supper is a time for anticipation and recommitment (1 Corinthians 11:26, 28–29).

UNLEAVENED BREAD

The Feast of Unleavened Bread commemorated Israel's hurried escape from Egypt. The unleavened bread (*matzah*) was made in a hurry without yeast, representing how the Lord brought the Israelites out of Egypt in haste. Leviticus 23:6 mentions the Feast of Unleavened Bread as a separate feast on the 15th day of the same month as Passover—*Nisan*. The Lord commanded the Israelites to eat unleavened bread for seven days.

Today the Feasts of Passover, Unleavened Bread, and Firstfruits have all been incorporated into the celebration of Passover. Passover is celebrated for eight days. In addition, the time of eating the bread became a time of spiritual preparation. Sometimes, leaven represents sin in the Bible. This feast also symbolizes a time of renewal and cleansing.

LEAVEN

- Leaven is something added to bread to make it rise (for example, yeast). Leaven requires time to expand.

- In Exodus 12:14–20 God commanded the Israelites to prepare unleavened bread as a way to remind them of the haste with which they had to leave Egypt.

- In those times, a leftover piece of fermented dough was used to make a new batch of dough rise. Today we use yeast to leaven the dough.

- Leaven is prohibited only at the Passover and in foods dedicated to the Lord by fire (Leviticus 2:11).

- In the Passover, removing leaven may represent a complete break from the previous life of slavery in Egypt and the coming into a new life under the Lord.

- However, for the peace offering (Leviticus 7:13) and the bread offered during Pentecost (Leviticus 23:17), leavened breads are required.

- This requirement suggests that in the Bible leaven does not always represent sin.

Unleavened Bread and Jesus

Because *matzah* is made without leaven, it can be a picture of Jesus. Since leaven often represents sin in the Scriptures, *matzah* may represent a pure life, a life without sin. Jesus is the only human without sin. In addition, Jesus said that the "bread of God is he who comes down from heaven and gives life to the world" (John 6:23). Jesus also declared, "I am the bread of life. He who comes to me will never go hungry" (John 6:35).

The symbolic links between Jesus and *matzah* can be extended to some characteristics of the bread. Today when *matzah* is made it is pierced—so the dough will not rise with the heat—and striped with marks made by the cook ware. (In the past, *matzah* looked like pita bread.) Many Jewish Christians understand the piercing and the stripes to symbolize the piercing of Jesus on the cross (John 19:34) and his flogging by the Roman soldiers (John 19:1).

Annibale Carracci

Fascinating Facts about the Feast of Unleavened Bread

- The only type of bread eaten during the eight days of Passover/Feast of Unleavened Bread was *matzah*.

- It is made with flour and water only, not leaven.

- It is striped and pierced during baking.

- The utensils used must never touch leaven.

- Bakery goods are made with matzo meal.

- Orthodox Jews believe that, during the feast, even having leaven present in one's home is forbidden.

Sterling Photo

- Today, cleansing the house the night before Passover is often a symbolic search to remove any hypocrisy or wickedness.

- Traditionally, the father searches for any leaven in the house. He sweeps any remaining bread crumbs onto a wooden spoon with a goose feather. The crumbs, spoon, and feather are placed in a bag and burned the next morning.

LEAVEN IN THE NEW TESTAMENT

- In the New Testament leaven may be used as a symbol of either good or bad influence.

- In Matthew 13:33 Jesus uses the image of leaven to explain the kingdom of heaven. Like leaven, the kingdom of heaven works unseen, powerfully, and relentlessly.

- In Luke 12:1, Jesus warns the disciples to beware of the Pharisees' teachings because, like leaven, they corrupt everything they touch.

- The Apostle Paul uses leaven imagery in 1 Corinthians 5:6–8 to emphasize the effect of bad influence: it spreads quickly and quietly. In other words, "malice and wickedness" corrupt everything just as leaven spreads and transforms the whole lump of bread.

- For Jews today, cleaning the house of yeast symbolizes getting rid of any sins in their lives. When a Jewish family prepares the home for the Passover celebration, they are required to search and remove any leaven from their house.

- This cleaning parallels the searching of the heart and repentance that Christians do when coming to the communion table.

FIRSTFRUITS

The Feast of Firstfruits was a reminder to Israel that God was the source of their prosperity and welfare. Firstfruits are offerings given for the spring barley harvest. The first ripe sheaf (firstfruits) of barley was offered to the Lord as an act of dedicating the harvest to him: an act of thanksgiving and commitment to God. On Passover, a marked sheaf of grain was bundled and left standing in the field. The next day was the first day of Unleavened Bread. It was on this day that the sheaf was cut and prepared for offering.

On the third day—the first day was the feasts of Passover, the second Unleavened Bread, and the third Firstfruits—the priest waved the sheaf before the Lord. The counting of the days (*omer*, which in Hebrew means "barley") then began and continued up to the day after the seventh Sabbath, the 50th day. The 50th day is called *shavuot* or Pentecost.

FIRSTFRUITS AND JESUS

After the destruction of the Temple in AD 70, Jewish people rarely celebrated Firstfruits. But it has great significance for followers of Jesus as the day of his resurrection—Easter. Jesus rose on the third day of Passover season, the day of Firstfruits (Luke 24:46–47). Jesus' resurrection gave new meaning to this agricultural holiday. Jesus' resurrection is the promise of the future resurrection of believers (1 Corinthians 15:20–23).

Photoexperience

LEVITICUS 23:9-14

The LORD said to Moses, "Speak to the Israelites and say to them: 'When you enter the land I am going to give you and you reap its harvest, bring to the priest a sheaf of the first grain you harvest. He is to wave the sheaf before the LORD so it will be accepted on your behalf; the priest is to wave it on the day after the Sabbath. On the day you wave the sheaf, you must sacrifice as a burnt offering to the LORD a lamb a year old without defect, together with its grain offering of two-tenths of an ephah of fine flour mixed with oil—an offering made to the LORD by fire, a pleasing aroma— and its drink offering of a quarter of a hin of wine. You must not eat any bread, or roasted or new grain, until the very day you bring this offering to your God. This is to be a lasting ordinance for the generations to come, wherever you live."

FASCINATING FACTS ABOUT THE FEAST OF FIRSTFRUITS

- Other biblical events that happened on this day:

    - The manna, which God provided from heaven as food for the Israelites while in the wilderness, stopped on this day after they entered the Promised Land.

    - Queen Esther risked her life on this day to save the Jewish people from annihilation.

- Since the temple was destroyed in AD 70, firstfruits are no longer offered on this day by Jewish people.

- Today, Jews use this holiday to begin the counting of the days, also known as the "counting of the omer" (an *omer* is a biblical measure of volume of grain).

- On the 33rd day of counting the *omer*, a minor rabbinical holiday also known by the Hebrew name *Lag Ba'Omer*, is celebrated.

1 CORINTHIANS 15:20–23

But Christ has indeed been raised from the dead, the firstfruits of those who have fallen asleep. For since death came through a man, the resurrection of the dead comes also through a man. For as in Adam all die, so in Christ all will be made alive. But each in his own turn: Christ, the firstfruits; then, when he comes, those who belong to him.

JAMES 1:16–18

Don't be deceived, my dear brothers. Every good and perfect gift is from above, coming down from the Father of the heavenly lights, who does not change like shifting shadows. He chose to give us birth through the word of truth, that we might be a kind of firstfruits of all he created.

FEAST OF WEEKS

*Count off seven weeks
from the time you begin
to put the sickle to the
standing grain. Then
celebrate the Feast of
Weeks to the LORD your
God by giving a freewill
offering in proportion
to the blessings the
LORD your God has
given you. And rejoice
before the LORD your
God at the place he will
choose as a dwelling for
his Name—you, your
sons and daughters,
your menservants and
maidservants, the Levites
in your towns, and the
aliens, the fatherless and
the widows living
among you.*

The Feast of Weeks, also known as *shavuot*, celebrates God's graceful provision of both material things and his Law. Traditionally, this celebration marks the culmination of the events that began with the Passover. It is an offering of grain of the summer wheat harvest presented to the Lord to show joy and thankfulness. Also known as the Feast of Harvest or Latter Firstfruits, it commemorates the giving of the Law at Sinai.

When the Temple was in existence, the Feast of Weeks was one of the three pilgrimage feasts. Passover and the Feast of Firstfruits were the other two. The Feast of *Shavuot* (which in Hebrew means *weeks*) is celebrated seven weeks from the celebration of the Feast of Firstfruits until the people arrived at Sinai. Because of this connection, the Feast is related to the giving of the *Torah* (the law). It is also known as "the Season of the Giving of Torah." It is believed that God gave Moses the Ten Commandments at this time.

K. Dmitry

FEAST OF WEEKS AND JESUS

After his resurrection, Jesus told his disciples to wait in Jerusalem. The disciples were all together in the upper room for *Shavuot* on the 50th day after the Sabbath of Passover week—the first day of the week.

Then the sound of a mighty wind filled the house and what appeared to be tongues of fire came to rest on the disciples, and they were filled with the Holy Spirit. The Apostle Peter referred to the prophet Joel who said that God would "pour out his Spirit on all flesh" (Joel 2:28-32). God was fulfilling his promises right before their eyes. Peter also said that the risen and exalted Jesus had poured out the Holy Spirit (Acts 2:32-33). The people responded to Peter's message and more than 3,000 were baptized that day.

Jean Restout

The Covenant between God and Israel was initiated on *Shavuot* at the foot of Mount Sinai, seven weeks after the Passover miracle in Egypt. On the day of Pentecost, fifty days after the death of Christ, the Spirit sealed the New Covenant in Jesus' blood (2 Corinthians 1:22; Ephesians 1:13; 4:30).

ACTS 2:1–4

When the day of Pentecost came, they were all together in one place. Suddenly a sound like the blowing of a violent wind came from heaven and filled the whole house where they were sitting. They saw what seemed to be tongues of fire that separated and came to rest on each of them. All of them were filled with the Holy Spirit and began to speak in other tongues as the Spirit enabled them.

FASCINATING FACTS ABOUT THE FEAST OF WEEKS

- *Shavuot* is celebrated 50 days after Passover, so it became known as Pentecost, meaning "50" in Greek.

- The days from Passover to *Shavuot* are counted at weekly Sabbath services.

- Historically, children receive treats for memorizing Scripture at *Shavuot*.

- The book of Ruth is often read.

- It is a popular day for Jewish Confirmation.

- Special dairy desserts are prepared for this holiday because the Law is compared to milk and honey.

- Homes and synagogues are decorated with flowers and greenery, representing the harvest and the *Torah* as a "tree of life."

- Observant Jews often spend the night reading and studying *Torah*.

FEAST OF TRUMPETS

The Feast of Trumpets is also called *Rosh HaShanah*, which means "the beginning of the year." It marks the beginning of the civil new year. It falls on the first day of the seventh month of the Hebrew calendar, *Tishrei*, which usually falls on September or October.

J. Steidl

In biblical times, it was a day of rest and offerings. It was commemorated with trumpet blasts. *Rosh Hashanah*, the Ten Days of Repentance that follow it, and then *Yom Kippur* make up the High Holy Days. Jewish tradition says that God writes every person's words, deeds, and thoughts in the book of life, which he opens on *Rosh Hashanah* (for the book of life, see Psalm 69:28). If good deeds outnumber sinful ones for the year, that person's name will be inscribed in the book of life for another year on *Yom Kippur*.

During *Rosh HaShanah* and the "Ten Days of Repentance," people can repent of their sins and do good deeds to increase their chances of being inscribed in the book of life.

LEVITICUS
23:23–25
The LORD said to Moses, "Say to the Israelites: 'On the first day of the seventh month you are to have a day of rest, a sacred assembly commemorated with trumpet blasts. Do no regular work, but present an offering made to the LORD by fire.'"

FEAST OF TRUMPETS AND JESUS

Rosh HaShanah is sometimes referred to as the Day of Judgment. Jesus said he has authority to judge people (John 5:24–27). Paul called Jesus the judge of "the living and the dead" (2 Timothy 4:1). God does have a book of life, the Lamb's book of life (Revelation 21:27). Doing good works does not get one's name written in the book of life (Titus 3:5–7). The only way to have one's name inscribed in this book of life is through faith in Jesus as Savior from sin. Of course, this does not free us from doing good works, "For we are God's workmanship, created in Christ Jesus to do good works, which God prepared in advance for us to do" (Ephesians 2:10).

PhotographerOlympus

1 CORINTHIANS 15:50–54

I declare to you, brothers, that flesh and blood cannot inherit the kingdom of God, nor does the perishable inherit the imperishable. Listen, I tell you a mystery: We will not all sleep, but we will all be changed— in a flash, in the twinkling of an eye, at the last trumpet. For the trumpet will sound, the dead will be raised imperishable, and we will be changed. For the perishable must clothe itself with the imperishable, and the mortal with immortality. When the perishable has been clothed with the imperishable, and the mortal with immortality, then the saying that is written will come true: "Death has been swallowed up in victory."

FASCINATING FACTS ABOUT THE FEAST OF TRUMPETS

- Prior to *Rosh HaShanah*, the shofar (ram's horn) is blown to call people to repent and remind them that the holy days are arriving.

- The shofar is blown 100 times during *Rosh HaShanah* synagogue services.

- *Rosh HaShanah* is a serious New Year holiday, not a happy one like January 1.

- A common custom is sending cards to relatives and friends to wish them a happy, healthy, and prosperous new year.

- The message includes the greeting *L'shanah tovah tikatevoo*, which means "May you be inscribed [in the Book of Life] for a good year."

- It is traditional to eat apple slices dipped in honey.

- The apples represent provision, and honey represents sweetness for the coming year.

Sterling Photo

Shofar made from a ram's horn

AwesomeShot Studios

DAY OF ATONEMENT

On the Day of Atonement, the high priest made atonement for sin in the Tabernacle or the Temple. It was the most solemn Jewish holy day. In Hebrew, *Yom* means "day"; *Kippur* means "atonement" or "covering." Atonement is God's way to bring reconciliation and restoration to the problem of human sin and its effects.

The 10 days between *Rosh HaShanah* and *Yom Kippur* are known as the Days of Repentance. *Yom Kippur* is the day of judgment when God judges the people. In biblical times, the high priest entered the Most Holy Place in the Tabernacle or Temple once a year on *Yom Kippur*. This was a time of fasting and prayer.

During *Yom Kippur*, the high priest brought two animals, usually goats, to the Tabernacle. He sacrificed one of the animals and offered the blood as a sacrifice of atonement on behalf of the people. This was an animal sacrifice to pay for his sins and the sins of the people. After the sacrifice, the high priest placed his hands on the other goat's head. He would pray asking for God's forgiveness for all the sins of the people. The sins of the people were transferred onto the goat. Then the animal was released into the wilderness. This "scapegoat" carried Israel's sins away, never to return.

LEVITICUS 16:29–34

"This is to be a lasting ordinance for you: On the tenth day of the seventh month you must deny yourselves and not do any work—whether native-born or an alien living among you—because on this day atonement will be made for you, to cleanse you. Then, before the LORD, you will be clean from all your sins. It is a sabbath of rest, and you must deny yourselves; it is a lasting ordinance. The priest who is anointed and ordained to succeed his father as high priest is to make atonement. He is to put on the sacred linen garments and make atonement for the Most Holy Place, for the Tent of Meeting and the altar, and for the priests and all the people of the community. This is to be a lasting ordinance for you: Atonement is to be made once a year for all the sins of the Israelites." And it was done, as the LORD commanded Moses.

THE DAY OF ATONEMENT AND JESUS

A thick veil from floor to ceiling separated the Most Holy Place in the Temple from the other rooms. When Jesus died on the cross, the veil was ripped from top to bottom. Christ came as high priest and entered the Most Holy Place once for all, by his own blood, having obtained eternal redemption (Hebrews 9:12). Believers in Jesus accept his sacrifice on the cross as the final atonement for sin. After the temple was destroyed in AD 70, Jewish people could no longer offer the sacrifices for atonement for sins. Today in many Jewish communities, repentance, prayers, and good works are seen as the means for obtaining atonement for sins.

Louis de Silvestre

Atonement for Sins				
	OLD COVENANT		**NEW COVENANT**	
Type of Sacrifice	Blood of Animals	Exodus 12:5 Leviticus 1–7	Blood of Jesus	Hebrews 9:12; 13:12 1 John 1:7
Quality of Sacrifice	Not enough Offered over and over	Leviticus 1–7 Hebrews 9:7–9; 10:4	Enough	Hebrews 9:12, 26
Quantity of Sacrifice	Many	Leviticus 1–7 Hebrews 10:1	One	Hebrews 9:25, 26
Effectiveness	For a day, for a year	Exodus 29–30 Hebrews 10:1–4	Forever	Hebrews 7:26, 27 Hebrews 9:12–15
Action or Result	Temporary	Exodus 30:10 Hebrews 9:25	Final	Romans 6:10 Hebrews 9:25–28

FASCINATING FACTS ABOUT THE DAY OF ATONEMENT

HEBREWS
9:26–28
*But now he has
appeared once
for all at the end
of the ages to do
away with sin by
the sacrifice of
himself. Just as
man is destined
to die once, and
after that to
face judgment,
so Christ was
sacrificed once to
take away the sins
of many people;
and he will
appear a second
time, not to bear
sin, but to bring
salvation to those
who are waiting
for him.*

- *Yom Kippur* is a day of fasting.

- No work is done on this day, including at home.

- Many Jewish people spend the day at synagogue, praying for forgiveness of their sins.

- The book of Jonah is read during the afternoon service to remind people of God's forgiveness and mercy.

- Immediately, after the evening service, participants have a "break-fast" meal.

THE FEAST OF TABERNACLES

The Feast of Tabernacles is a reminder of the 40-year wilderness journey. It is a call to remember God's faithfulness and protection during the journey. During the wilderness journey, the Israelites dwelt in temporary shelters, or booths (*sukkot*). During this holiday, the Israelites were to build and dwell in booths for seven days to remember how they had lived under God's care in the wilderness. It was a week-long celebration of the fall harvest. Along with Passover and Pentecost, the Feast of Tabernacles was one of the three pilgrimage feasts.

Israel became an agricultural society. The cycles of the land were important for biblical Israel. From

J. Maree

an agricultural perspective, Passover corresponded to the planting season, Pentecost corresponded to the grain harvest, and Tabernacles corresponded to the fruit harvest.

There are three things required for the Feast of Tabernacles, also known as Festival of *Sukkot*:

- To gather the "four species" (Leviticus 23:40). The four special plants used to cover the booths are myrtle, citron, palm, and willow.

- To live in a *sukkah* or booth (Leviticus 23:42).

- To rejoice before the Lord (Deuteronomy 16:13–14; Leviticus 23:40).

THE FEAST OF TABERNACLES AND JESUS

Two ceremonies were part of the last day:

- A priest carried water from the pool of Siloam to the Temple, symbolizing that when the Messiah comes the whole earth will know God "as the waters cover the sea." (Isaiah 11:9)

- People carrying torches marched around the temple, then set these lights around the walls of the temple, symbolizing how the Messiah would be a light to the Gentiles.

When Jesus attended this feast, on the last day, he said, "If anyone is thirsty, let him come to me and drink. Whoever believes in me… streams of living water will flow from within him" (John 7:37-38). The next morning, while the torches were still burning, he said, "I am the light of the world. Whoever follows me will never walk in darkness, but will have the light of life" (John 8:12). This feast represents the final harvest when all nations will share in the joy and blessings of God's kingdom. During that time, all believers will celebrate this feast (Zechariah 14:16).

FASCINATING FACTS ABOUT THE FEAST OF TABERNACLES

- *Sukkot* is a joyous feast when people rejoice in God's forgiveness and material blessings.

- Jews continue to celebrate *Sukkot* by building temporary booths for eight days.

- The *sukkah*, or booth, is a temporary structure built of wood, or wood and canvas.

- The *sukkah* is decorated with fall flowers, leaves, fruits, and vegetables.

- The *sukkah* is usually erected on a lawn or balcony.

- Often at least one meal a day is eaten in the *sukkah*.

- The *lulav* is a bouquet made of the palm branches, myrtle and willow branches that are bound together and waved/shaken in praise to the LORD.

- The *lulav* is waved in all four directions (north, south, east, and west) and up and down to symbolize that God's presence is everywhere.

LEVITICUS 23:40–43

On the first day you are to take choice fruit from the trees, and palm fronds, leafy branches and poplars, and rejoice before the LORD your God for seven days. Celebrate this as a festival to the LORD for seven days each year. This is to be a lasting ordinance for the generations to come; celebrate it in the seventh month. Live in booths for seven days: All native-born Israelites are to live in booths so your descendants will know that I had the Israelites live in booths when I brought them out of Egypt. I am the LORD your God.

Other Rose Bestselling Bible Reference Books

Rose Book of Bible Charts, Volume 1

Enjoy this best-selling book expanded with new charts, upgraded maps highlighting modern-day cities and countries, and up-to-date facts and statistics! Includes 216 reproducible pages of illustrations, charts, and maps on a variety of Bible topics, with two fold-outs of the genealogy of Jesus, cutaway Tabernacle illustration and Bible Time Line.
Hardcover. 229 pages. ISBN: 9781596360228

Rose Book of Bible Charts, Volume 2

Topics include • Bible Translations comparison chart • Why Trust the Bible • Heroes of the Old Testament • Women of the Bible • Life of Paul • Christ in the Old Testament • Christ in the Passover • Names of Jesus • Beatitudes • Lord's Prayer • Where to Find Favorite Bible Verses • Christianity and Eastern Religions • Worldviews Comparison • 10 Q & A on Mormonism/Jehovah's Witnesses/Magic/Atheism and many others!
Hardcover. 240 pages. ISBN: 9781596362758

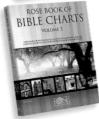

Rose Book of Bible Charts, Volume 3

Topics include • Who I Am in Christ (Assurance of Salvation) • What the Bible Says about Forgiveness • What the Bible Says about Money • What the Bible Says about Prayer • Spiritual Disciplines • Heaven • Attributes of God • How to Explain the Gospel • Parables of Jesus • Bible Character Studies and many more! Hardcover. 240 pages. ISBN: 9781596368699

Rose Book of Bible & Christian History Time Lines

Six thousand years and 20 feet of time lines in one hard-bound cover! These gorgeous time lines printed on heavy chart paper, can also be slipped out of their binding and posted in a hallway or large room for full effect. The Bible Time Line compares Scriptural events with world history and Middle East history. The Christian History Time Line begins with the life of Jesus and continues to the present day. Includes key people and events that all Christians should know. Hardcover. ISBN: 9781596360846

Rose Chronological Guide to the Bible

Look at the Bible in a fresh new way by viewing Bible events in the order they happened. It includes • Three 24-inch chronology foldouts showing the Bible at a glance, the life of Jesus, and the kings and prophets of the Old Testament • Chronology charts on popular Bible topics • Maps showing the journeys of the patriarchs, the exodus route, where Jesus walked, Paul's missionary trips. • Quick summaries of all sixty-six books of the Bible and when they happened. Hardcover. 178 pages. ISBN: 9781628628074

Rose Then and Now® Bible Map Atlas
with Biblical Background and Culture

Your 30 favorite Bible characters come alive with this new Bible atlas. Find out how the geography of Bible Lands affected the culture and decisions of people such as David, Abraham, Moses, Esther, Deborah, Jonah, Jesus, and the disciples. Hardcover. 272 pages. ISBN: 9781596365346

Rose Guide to the Tabernacle

Full color with clear overlays and reproducible pages. Learn how the sacrifices, utensils, and even the structure of the tabernacle were designed to show us something about God. See the parallels between the Old Testament sacrifices and priests' duties, and Jesus' service as the perfect sacrifice and perfect high priest. See how • The Tabernacle was built • The sacrifices pointed Jesus Christ • The design of the tent revealed God's holiness and humanity's need for God • The Ark of the Covenant was at the center of worship. Hardcover. 128 pages. ISBN: 9781596362765

Deluxe Then and Now® Bible Maps

Connect the "Middle East" of the news with the Holy Land in Scripture! Clear plastic overlays show modern cities and countries on top of Bible maps relevant to the patriarchs, Jesus, Paul, and the early church. Expanded edition includes 30 new pages of charts, illustrations, diagrams, and more.. Hardcover. ISBN: 9781628628593

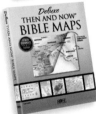

Rose Guide to the Temple

Simply the best book on the Temple in Jerusalem. It is the only full-color book from a Christian viewpoint that has clear plastic overlays showing the interior and exterior of Solomon's Temple, Herod's Temple, and the Tabernacle. Contains more than 100 color diagrams, photos, illustrations, maps, and time lines of more than 100 key events from the time of King David to modern day. It also includes two full-color posters: the Temple of Jesus' time and the stunning National Geographic poster on the Temple Mount through time. Hardcover. 144 pages. ISBN: 9781596364684

Jesus' Family Tree
Seeing God's Faithfulness in the Genealogy of Christ

Packed with time lines, family trees, and simple summaries, this incredible reference book gives a fantastic overview of 30 key people in Jesus' ancestry. The remarkable heroes and heroines in the ancestry of Jesus teach us a lot about God's faithfulness over the centuries. Each character in Jesus' family tree gives us a glimpse of how God works all things—even the tragedies and missteps—together for good. Hardcover. 192 pages ISBN: 9781628620085

www.HendricksonRose.com